ILLINOIS STATE MILITIA.

HEAD QUARTERS,

Springfield, Ills., _____ October 23. 1861

To all to whom These Presents Shall come, Greeting:

Know Ye, That *Ulysses S. Grant* having been duly

appointed Colonel of the Twenty First Regiment Illinois Volunteers.

I, RICHARD YATES,

Governor of the State of Illinois, and Commander-in-Chief of the Illinois State Militia,

FOR AND ON BEHALF OF THE PEOPLE OF SAID STATE, DO COMMISSION HIM TO TAKE

Rank as *Colonel* from the *Fifteenth* day of *June* 1861

He is, therefore, carefully and diligently to discharge the duties of said Office, by doing and performing all manner of things thereunto belonging; and I do strictly require all Officers and Soldiers under his command to be obedient to his orders; and he is to obey all such orders and directions as he shall receive, from time to time, from his Commander-in-Chief, or superior Officer.

In Testimony Whereof, I have hereunto set my hand and caused the GREAT SEAL OF STATE to be affixed.

Done at the City of Springfield, this *Twenty third* day of *October* in the year of our Lord one thousand eight hundred and sixty-*One* and of the independence of the United States, the eighty-*Sixth.*

BY THE GOVERNOR:

Rich. Yates
Commander-in-Chief, Illinois Militia.

O. M. Hatch
Secretary of State.

Registered in Vol. A, Page 77 *Thomas S. Mather*
Adjutant General, I. S. M.

Grant's 1861 Illinois Commission reproduced through the courtesy of the Armed Forces History Division of the Smithsonian Institution.

CONVERSATIONS

WITH

GENERAL GRANT

An Informal Biography
by Thomas G. McConnell

Walnut Hill Publishing Company
Annandale, Virginia

First Edition. All Rights Reserved
Published by Walnut Hill Publishing Company
Post Office Box 1395
Annandale, Virginia 22003-1395
Editor for Walnut Hill Publishing: Dona Dickinson.
Cover and jacket design by Kevin Osborn of Research & Design Associates
Printed in the United States of America.

Grateful acknowledgment is made for permission to quote from:
GRANT MOVES SOUTH by Bruce Catton. Copyright 1960 by Little, Brown & Co.
WITH MALICE TOWARD NONE by Stephen B. Oates. Copyright 1977 by Stephen B. Oates. Published by Harper & Row, Publishers, Inc.
10 9 8 7 6 5 4 3 2 1

Library of Congress Cataloging in Publication Data
McConnell, Thomas G. (Thomas Grant), date.
Conversations with General Grant : an informal biography / by Thomas G. McConnell. -- 1st ed.
p. cm.
Includes bibliographical references.
ISBN 1-878332-11-2 : $19.95. -- ISBN 1-878332-10-4 (pbk.) : $9.95
1. Grant, Ulysses S. (Ulysses Simpson), 1822-1885--Military leadership. 2. Generals--United States--Biography. 3. United States. Army--Biography. 4. United States--History--Civil War, 1861-1865--Campaigns. I. Title.
E672.M13 1990
973.8'2'092--dc20
[B]   89-29620
                                                              CIP

DEDICATION

DEDICATED to the millions of men and women who served and the hundreds of thousands who died to preserve this arsenal of freedom we call the United States of America --- particularly to those soldier-ancestors of whom I am aware: My greatgrandfather, Private William Wheat, 154th New York Volunteers, 1862 - 1866; my grandfather, Regimental Quartermaster John McConnell, 6th Cavalry Regiment, U.S. Army, 1867 - 1897; and most of all to my father, Corporal Samuel H. McConnell, AEF 1917 - 1918 --- a man whose stride I'll never match and whose shoes I'll never fill.

> **The muffled drum's sad roll has beat**
> **The soldier's last tattoo;**
> **No more on life's parade shall meet**
> **That brave and fallen few.**
> **On Fame's eternal camping ground**
> **Their silent tents are spread**
> **And Glory guards with solemn round,**
> **The bivouac of the dead.**

Excerpted from *BIVOUAC OF THE DEAD* by Theodore O'Hara. (National Cemetery, Sharpsburg - Antietam Battlefield Park, Maryland).

Acknowledgments

The most important contribution which I must acknowledge is that of my wife, Pat, for hers is the *sine qua non* of the entire effort. In the days before personal computers were a household item, she drudged over a balky portable to produce the many drafts, revisions and then the final copy of my original work on Grant --- a special project for the Air Command and Staff College. In addition, I want to thank her for her suggestion and inspiration to re-work *GENERAL GRANT* into a publishable format and her more recent encouraging words despite the frustrations of paper-littered rooms and the seemingly endless hammering of that house-shaking IBM Selectric.

My very special thanks go to Dr. Jay Luvaas of the Army War College. Dr. Luvaas lectured enthrallingly to my history of warfare class at The National War College. He took the Civil War out of musty archives and made it a living and relevant thing for nuclear age warriors. On a personal level, he introduced me to a singular technique for viewing Civil War battlefields. Under his tutelage, I discovered how to make silent scenes seem to come alive again with the roar of battle, the acrid smell of burnt gunpowder and the everpresent fog of war --- to see them now just as Grant, Lee and the others lived them one hundred and twenty-five years ago.

I truly appreciate the outstanding assistance provided by Dona Dickinson of Walnut Hill Publishing and Elaine Hollar, Dona's computer specialist compatriot at NETWORK ADVANTAGE of Springfield, Virginia. Without their knowledge of computer assisted book publishing this book may not have come to pass. Beyond the technical aspects, Dona was the indispensable element for this version of

General Grant's story. She established the format, produced the maps, did much of the editing and provided a good deal of moral support as this work progressed.

My sons, Patrick, Tom, and Kevin as well as my daughters-in-law Lynda and Brenda have also earned my gratitude for volunteering their special expertise for the very time consuming job of editing and reediting the text. In addition, I am particularly grateful for their advice on improving the book as well as their technical inputs. Their assistance was sorely needed, actively sought and greatly appreciated as we readied this volume for the printer.

I want to thank several of my long time friends and former colleagues for their moral support as I struggled on with General Grant: Colonels George Wish and Harry Dunn, USAF (Ret) whom I have known for so long that it seems our friendships might have begun in a previous life; from The National War College, Dr. John Bennett --- still a fellow traveller to the battlefields; Colonel Donald Mahley, U. S. Army, whose give and take on military subjects has always been inspiring and Colonel Frank J. (Mick) McKeown, USAF, who, I am sure, would have flogged me had I not completed "Conversations with General Grant." I also must thank Dr. Paul Malone of the George Washington University, Colonel U. S. Army, Retired, and the author and publisher of "Love 'Em and Lead 'Em," for his invaluable "poynters" on how to bring this work to fruition. Then there is a certain friend who flew with me often in Vietnam and, from wherever he may be, never forgets to telephone his own words of encouragement: Brian Daly.

To the many other friends --- including Bastian (Buz) Hello, Jim Anderson, Maria Hoffmann, John & Esther Ford, Tom & Dottie Hopper --- who also have an appreciation for the suffering the American people endured over a century ago and who have been willing to share their thoughts with me as we tramped battlefields together, I also say thanks.

CONTENTS

Introduction 15

Chapter One: 17
"General Scott visited West Point and reviewed the cadets ... I believe I did have a presentiment for a moment that some day I should occupy his place on review."
PROLOGUE

Chapter Two: 27
"My name is Ulysses Grant and I'm an alcoholic, or am I ?"
THE ENEMY WITHIN

Chapter Three: 44
"Please call me by the only nickname I like: General!"....
FROM HIRAM TO "UNCONDITIONAL SURRENDER"

Chapter Four: 79
"... To walk on dead bodies without a foot touching the ground."
SHILOH

Chapter Five: 96
"I was on dry ground on the same side of the river with the enemy."
THE VICKSBURG CAMPAIGN

Chapter Six: 118
"The specticle [sic] was grand beyond anything that has been or is likely to be on this continent."
CHATTANOOGA

Chapter Seven: 136
"*That may all be well, but Bobby Lee is waiting just across the Rapidan.*"
VIRGINIA, 1864

Chapter Eight: 170
"*I think it is pretty well to get across a great river and come up here and attack Lee before he is ready for us.*"
PETERSBURG

Chapter Nine: 190
"*I was still suffering from the ... headache; but the instant I saw Lee's note I was cured.*"
THE ROAD TO APPOMATTOX!

Chapter Ten: 203
Papa Grant, Bobby Lee, and other ghosts from the past!
A DESPERATE NEED.

Chapter Eleven: 220
"*I propose fight it out ... if it takes all summer --- again.*"
THE FIGHT AGAINST POVERTY AND CANCER

Bibliography 230

Index 232

Author's Biograhpy 237

Order Sheets

MAPS

Grant's Moves in the West (September 1861 - April 1862)   95
Vicksburg Campaign (April - July 1861)   110
Chattanooga (October - November 1863)   126
Spottsylvania (May 10, 1864)   151
Spottsylvania (May 12, 1864)   153
Spottsylvania (May 13 - 14, 1864)   155
Spottsylvania (May 17 - 18, 1864)   157
Spottsylvania (May 19 - 20, 1864)   159
North Anna River (May 24, 1864)   161
Pursuit to Appomattox (April 3 - 9, 1865)   192

INTRODUCTION

Several years ago, while a student at the Air Force's Command and Staff College, I was asked to write an extensive biography of General Grant. My colleagues, uno voce, wondered why the faculty wanted me to write about a drunkard. More recently, I was touring the Richmond battlefields on which Lee's Army of Northern Virginia and the Army of the Potomac collided. The group included several senior army officers, who argued that a drinker like Grant had no business thinking that he could wage a successful campaign against the military genius of Robert E. Lee. There was no recognition that the engagement in Virginia was the part of Grant's larger strategic plan under which, for the first time, all the armies moved in concert, or that it was essential to keep Lee so tightly engaged that the other armies could perform unhindered by his daring maneuvers, or that several times during the campaign the Army of the Potomac actually had tactical advantages over its opponent but was unable to make anything of them. No! The verdict was in: "He drank" --- and that said it all.

What I hope to do in this book is to provide the reader with some insights into the true Grant, not just the legends of the drinking bouts. His is an amazing success story, and had he not been successful it is very likely that the United States would not be the same nation that we know today.

Certainly, he had his flaws, including an occasional bout with the bottle, but these should not be allowed to overshadow his accomplishments. Even his Presidency, so often used as a bludgeon by his detractors, had many bright and some brilliant spots. It must be said, though, that Grant was neither a politician nor a businessman. In fact, in the hands of politicians and financiers he was victimized like a waif in a Charles Dickens novel.

I've called this an informal biography in contrast to a scholarly work replete with supported analyses and extensive documentation. However, the narrative is not simply the product of an overactive imagination. It is based on serious study of Grant over the years and heavy involvement in the writings of his colleagues, his formal biographers, general Civil War histories, the musty volumes of the *OFFICIAL RECORDS OF THE WAR OF THE REBELLION*, and the General's highly readable and informative, even if slightly biased, *MEMOIRS*. This approach gives me more freedom than the scholar is allowed. Like a historical novelist, I can present conclusions derived from extensive study of the facts, but without the necessity of being slavishly dependent on the previously written word. End result? An opportunity for the reader to get to know and understand the man rather than the myth --- to appreciate why no less a personage than General William Tecumseh Sherman said of him:

Each epoch creates its own agents, and General Grant more nearly than any other impersonated the American character of 1861-1865. He will stand, therefore, as the typical hero of the great Civil War.

CHAPTER ONE

"GENERAL SCOTT VISITED WEST POINT AND REVIEWED THE CADETS ... I BELIEVE I DID HAVE A PRESENTIMENT FOR A MOMENT THAT SOME DAY I SHOULD OCCUPY HIS PLACE ON REVIEW"

PROLOGUE

Four hundred years ago, Shakespeare wrote, "All the world's a stage and all the men and women merely players. They have their exits and their entrances." As Shakespeare's timeless play of life unfolds, there are those whom the gods, it seems, have predestined to step onto his world stage at a precise moment in history. Thus, at that entrance cue prescribed by the Fates, a Churchill, MacArthur, Washington, Roosevelt or Robert E. Lee strides into history's spotlight.

But Shakespeare's play also has a place for life's understudies, those who unexpectedly find themselves sharing applause with the exalted stars. Thus the mantle of enduring greatness fell on Joan of Arc, an illiterate peasant girl who guided the destinies of France; Napoleon, who burst from the turmoil of revolution to dominate Europe for over a decade; and Abraham Lincoln, elected to immortality by a nation torn by the issue of human bondage. To these we may add Ulysses Simpson Grant, who rose from a Bob Crachit existence in his father's leather shop to become the leader of the most powerful military force the world had then known.

Ulysses Simpson Grant --- whose very name was a mistake, yet the President of the United States chose him to lead his armies.

Porter.   Marshall.   Sheridan.
                                                          Ingalls.
                                                          Babcock.   Custer.

Lee.   Grant.   Merritt.
                                             Parker.

GRANT AT APPOMATTOX.

Ulysses Simpson Grant--- who just ten years before was branded a drunkard and resigned from the Army in disgrace, yet Congress conferred upon him a military rank previously held only by George Washington. Ulysses Simpson Grant --- whose wartime service began preparing enlistment forms in a state militia office and ended with his inauguration as the nation's 18th president.

Few among those who met him, as the decade of the 1850's was coming to a close, would have predicted that this seedy St. Louis cordwood salesman in the faded blue overcoat had the spark of greatness within him. By 1861, even the farm which provided the wood was gone and he, a $2.00 a day clerk, huddled pitifully in a corner of his father's store. It was during these hard times that his domineering father would look at his offspring with disdain and rant, "West Point ruined my son for business." Yet it had been this mocking parent who had forced his firstborn to accept an appointment to West Point. Grant would not escape from the darkness of his taunting father's shadow until just a few days before the general's agonizingly painful death in 1885.

As the 1860's began, cataclysmic events were erupting which would shake the United States to her very foundation. Manifest Destiny had been the nation's driving force for two decades and it produced a nation which spanned the continent. With the 1860 election of Abraham Lincoln, however, Manifest Destiny faded into the background as the long dormant ghost of secession wailed its portents of disaster across the land. During the next four years a divided people struggled mercilessly to determine whether the concept of "one nation indivisible" was merely an ephemeral gathering of independent states. Through 1861, 1862, and 1863 the battles raged and the guns roared. Again and again the armies marched to the Temple of Mars to leave their bloody sacrifices.

At the end the two sides had placed 650,000 silent offerings on the altars of the insatiable gods as they battled to determine whether this government of the people, by the people, shall or shall not perish from the earth.

Despite this incredible slaughter, neither side had been able to impose its will on the other as the third bloody year of war ended. The autumn of 1863 became the winter of 1864, and the armies in Blue and in Gray watched defiantly --- both sides waiting for the tocsin to sound for the next wave of violence.

In the early years of the war, both sides produced their Titans among men: Robert E. Lee in the South --- a general who came within a hairsbreadth of stealing victory from a war weary North --- Abraham Lincoln in the North --- one of the few men willing to pay the price for a lasting Union and who suffered the dagger slashes of a thousand Brutuses as he solidified the mettle of his countrymen. About to join this august company as the year 1864 unfolded was Ulysses S. Grant. What Lincoln had been in bolstering the spirit of the people, Grant would become in forging the iron backbone of a million fighting men.

"Who is this Grant?" thousands rightfully asked. At the beginning of the war only two people seemed aware of him at all, and both of these were Confederates: James Longstreet, the Commanding General of Lee's 1st Corps, a year ahead of Grant at West Point and at one time a very close friend, and Richard Ewell, Stonewall Jackson's replacement as 2nd Corps Commander in Lee's army. "There is one West Pointer," Ewell wrote in 1861, "I mean in Missouri, whom I hope the Northern people will not find out. I mean Sam Grant. I knew him well at the Academy, and in Mexico. I should fear him more than any of their officers I have yet heard of. He is not a man of genius, but he is clearheaded, quick and daring." So anonymous was Grant at the beginning of the war, that historian Bruce Catton did not have a single entry about him in *The Coming Fury,* the first volume of his Civil War trilogy. To the people in and out of the military he was virtually an unknown, and those who had heard of him it usually focused on a single piece of notoriety: "He drank".

Let's take a brief look at the background of this almost overlooked soldier who proved to be Lincoln's man of steel. Grant was born in Ohio, the son of Hannah Simpson and Jesse Grant. His father was self educated, a writer and poet of some note, and a business success --- something Grant would never be nor could his father ever understand. Named Hiram Ulysses at birth, the family called him Ulysses --- but to his chagrin, playmates often tabbed him as "Useless" or "Lyss." He appears to have been a sensitive youngster who could vividly recall the taunts of the other children and his father's chastisements even when he was on his deathbed. Thus, when the monogram H.U.G. appeared on his luggage as he was about to leave for West Point, his name quickly became Ulysses Hiram. However, when the officials at the Point told him his name was Ulysses Simpson (an error on the part of the appointing Congressman) he typically became the master of the predicament and adopted his new and everlasting name.

At West Point he had a nondescript career, finishing in the middle of the class in academics and demerits, doing well in mathematics and excelling in horsemanship. In the Mexican War he served with both Zachary Taylor and Winfield Scott, received minor accolades as well as two promotions for his courage and his military aptitude. After the war he married Julia Dent. She was the sister of his West Point roommate, Frederick Dent, and came from the landed gentry of St. Louis, Missouri. For two years all went well as they enjoyed assignments in Michigan and New York. He had expected to return to West Point as a professor of mathematics, but instead found himself on a steamer bound for an outpost in Oregon Territory.

The $677 annual pay of a junior officer would never make ends meet on the West Coast, so he left Julia and their two infants behind. For two years he was miserable.

He tried several business ventures to supplement his pay but each was an abysmal failure. A transportation delay turned an ice delivery service into warm water; a potato farm was inundated by the flooding Columbia River; a chicken raising enterprise perished as the chickens died before arriving at market. Lonely, deprived of fast horses --- his only pleasure other than his family --- burdened with an assignment which may have lasted for God-only-knew-how-long, young Grant took to drink. He was finally given a choice: Resign or face a court-martial. In 1854, Grant began the seven years of civilian life which would end in his father's store.

The Civil War came and Grant expected that he, as a West Pointer, would be in demand. Not so ! "Sam Grant was a drunk," the old army grapevine said. George McClellan, then a major-general in Ohio, ignored him; the Washington government never bothered to respond to his application. He did help Governor Yates of Illinois to raise militia companies, but he fully expected that he would soon be back in the leather shop --- deemed unworthy to serve his country in its most desperate hour of need. Then the Fates dealt him a new hand.

In June of 1861, a rowdy militia regiment of 30-day volunteers needed a commander to bring them under control and to convince them to extend their enlistments to three years. In despair, Governor Yates reached out to the only man he knew who had some experience in these matters --- the drab little man from Galena who worked at a broken desk in one of the outer offices.

"Captain Grant, will your take this assignment?"

"Yes, Sir, I will."

And a legend was born.

The regiment reenlisted and in a few months Grant had a political appointment as a brigadier-general and the command of a military district. Within six months the new general had moved his troops into Paducah, Kentucky and captured the Confederate's Fort Henry. He quickly followed these victories with the conquest of Fort Donelson --- and was suddenly being hailed throughout the land as "Unconditional Surrender" Grant.

The old Army, however, couldn't stand this upstart who scored victories by scoffing at the conventional rules of warfare. The grapevine began to hum again: "Grant drinks!" Lincoln countered: "Grant fights!" and promoted him ahead of all others to major-general.

After the bloodbath at Shiloh, where Grant and his army were caught off-guard, the backbiting began again. This time it nearly drove Grant to resign, but Lincoln reminded his warlords: "Grant wins." On to Vicksburg, but as he slogged through the winter's mud in vain attempts to find a dry foothold on which to fight the enemy, the chorus broke into song once more: "Grant drinks, Grant was drinking, Grant was drunk."

Lincoln's faith wavered, but in the end he stood by his fighting general. In the Spring, Grant found his dry ground and in three weeks, after conducting what still may be the most audacious campaign in U.S. military history, he had thirty thousand Confederates bottled up within the confines of Vicksburg. Then Lincoln is reported to have joked about getting Grant's brand of liquor for the other Union generals.

It was now Grant's turn to be Lincoln's savior. From Vicksburg the troubled Lincoln sent him to Chattanooga. He was ordered to rescue General Rosecrans' Army of the Cumberland from the Confederate siege imposed after the battle of Chickamauga.

Some three weeks after his arrival, Grant ordered a combined army group to attack the Confederates' seemingly impregnable position. Two days of bitter fighting ensued. Finally, Bragg's Army of Tennessee was in headlong flight toward Atlanta and Lincoln was on the verge of giving to Grant the supreme command of the Armies of the United States.

In three months, the stodgy quartermaster of the Mexican War, the disgrace of the old army, the failure in prewar civilian life, would be wearing shoulder straps which only the "Father of his Country" had worn before him. In five months, he would send the combined armies wheeling southward in a last ditch attempt to wring the life from the Rebellion. Less than a year later, he would sit at a small table in the McLean House at Appomattox and scrawl out a note to General Lee which would once more give meaning to the motto "*E Pluribus Unum*".

Shakespeare also wrote: "Some are born to greatness, some achieve greatness, some have greatness thrust upon them." What should we say about a man who in just four years moved from being an object of his father's charity to being the general to whom a grieving President turned in the forlorn hope of saving the Union? About one of life's failures who engineered the final victory after so many who were seemingly born to greatness had failed? Who commanded forces more powerful than the world had ever seen to that time? Who was never defeated in battle? Who personally accepted the surrender of three opposing armies; oversaw the surrender of two additional armies; and in the end brought down the entire hostile government? Should we say that he achieved greatness despite the odds stacked against him or was it that Lincoln, in desperation, thrust greatness upon him? The answers may be academic; however, in granting him a measure of greatness one must also concede that his greatness was one dimensional. The truth is that whenever Grant strayed from the military environment, mediocrity hounded him.

In this regard, we have already seen his ineptitude in business before the Civil War and we will later look at his dismal stint as a Wall Street financier. Similarly, sincere historians grade his Presidency as among the worst in the country's history. Since these conversations focus on Grant the general and not his performance as President, it is sufficient to say here that politics was as unfriendly to Grant as business had been. Time and time again he was hoodwinked by people whom he had regarded as personal friends.

In fairness, however, as President he did have several personal triumphs which are usually lost in the noise about the scandals which wracked his administration. For instance, he pushed for civil service reform and actually had a Civil Service Commission in being for four years. Unfortunately, it took President Garfield's assassination to prove to Congress that Grant was right. He was also responsible for forging an accommodation with a hostile England which resulted in the Treaty of Washington. The treaty settled the dispute over the damages perpetrated by the British privateers during the war, fixed the boundary between the United States and Canada on terms favorable to the United States and settled a long-standing fight over fishing rights in British-American waters.

Grant's personal honesty as a public official, moreover, has been well verified and he often used the power of his office to thwart the thieving scoundrels. It should be said, however, that Grant's administration appears as a confused slough with just an occasional glimmer of light. The confusion, unfortunately, left a stain on Grant's reputation which endures to the present day.

Perhaps now it's time to meet General Grant.

CHAPTER TWO

"MY NAME IS ULYSSES GRANT AND I AM AN ALCOHOLIC* - OR AM I?"

THE ENEMY WITHIN

SYNOPSIS: As mentioned before, Grant's reputation as a drinker seems to have outlived and overwhelmed the record of his invaluable contributions to the Union cause. However, it is not only in the history books that he suffers, the stain of insobriety also affected him in his own day. As we noted, only a governor's desperate need brought this indispensable man into the service. Does "indispensable" overstate Grant's case? I don't think so. When Lincoln turned to Grant in 1864, there was no other Union general who had demonstrated consistent battlefield success. Had Grant not succeeded, the map of the North American continent may have developed far differently from what we see today. And let us not forget that Grant, with a devoted host ready to do his bidding, never challenged the concept of civilian control of the military --- not an insignificant attribute in the era of the "Man on a White Horse."

With this background, we should acknowledge or dismiss the charges of Grant's drinking early on. That's why it is the subject of our first conversation.

*--- As defined by the American Heritage dictionary, 1981 New College Edition: "A chronic pathological condition, chiefly of the nervous and gastroenteric systems, caused by habitual excessive alcoholic consumption."

No, General Grant, you're not an alcoholic. A drinker? Yes! Sometimes you took more than was wise? Yes! But an alcoholic? No! You know, General, I do have to say that it's a fair question. No matter when or where the Civil War is being discussed, the subject inevitably turns to General Grant and drinking.

....

Maybe it isn't right, General, but it's true. A few years ago, I was working on a study of your military leadership and people who should have known better wondered why I was wasting my time writing about a "boozer." They had no comments about Donelson, Shiloh, Vicksburg, or Chattanooga --- just, "Why write about a drunk?" Later I was at Cold Harbor and again people who should have known better were arguing about your sobriety when you ordered the Cold Harbor attack.

....

You can say that I must be wrong all that you want, but that's the way things are. That's why I think it's time to talk openly about "Grant the Boozer", "Grant the Drunk" and "Grant the Alcoholic". Don't look at me that way. I said openly and I meant it. You've never done that before, you know. You certainly didn't mention the subject in your *MEMOIRS,* nor did Julia say much about drinking in her reminiscences. Yes! I think it's about time that you opened up on the subject.

....

All right, you can say that you didn't think that it was important, but I think that both you and Julia were trying to sweep the whole thing under the rug.

....

Now look, General, you've been dead for over a hundred years and even you have to admit that liquor is still a stain on your reputation. Good grief, Man, virtually every biographer or Civil War historian makes an issue of your drinking. Bruce Catton, as he finished the final two volumes of the biography

Lloyd Lewis began, brought up the subject no less than fifteen times.

.... ?

That's what I said, General, fifteen times.

....

No, that's not an isolated case. There's William McFeely. In his recent biography, *GRANT*, he had seventeen entries on "drinking habits." Even the revered Carl Sandburg brought up the matter nine times --- and remember, he was writing about Abraham Lincoln, not Grant. I could go on, but I think that you get the point: It's not a trivial matter and it's about time we talked frankly about Grant and liquor.

.... ?

How are we going to do it? Well, I'll tell you. I mentioned Catton, McFeely and Lewis already, and there were many others who looked deeply into this subject. Some of these writers were your compatriots, others lived during the war and chronicled the events, many are more recent students of the Civil War. We're going to take a look at what they said about you and alcohol --- and set the record straight once and for all. Let's go back to Mexico during the Mexican War --- that's where we see the first signs of this drinking business. Lt. Sam Grant ...

....?

Well, your friends called you Sam back then --- and many people still do --- with a group of other young officers and plenty of time on your hands. What would we expect? A little hell raising was the order of the day. Lloyd Lewis went into great detail.

... ...?

No, General, he didn't say that you were the only one --- he was talking about soldiers in general. He claimed that they were always drunk; they robbed, stole, even killed for their own amusement and they bought too much "pulque."

....

Yes, I'll be that it's been a long time since you heard that word. Pulque --- similar to tequila but distilled from the agave plant, it must have been potent stuff. But there you were, young men away from home, not much activity ...

....

Hey! I agree. It's not unusual for the gang to sit around and "tip" a few. But are you sure that it was just a few? And just occasionally? Then how come you became a charter member of the Sackett Harbor Sons of Temperance after you returned from Mexico?

Nothing to say? I think that we both know that there was a sound reason for you to join the "fraternal order." William Woodward, when writing *MEET GENERAL GRANT*, did a good deal of research into this phase of your life. He described how you began drinking in Mexico and "... whisky was humming in your soul..." and that your new bride, Julia, encouraged you to take the pledge.

....

Don't bark at me, General. My God, you'll wake the dead. I didn't say those things about you, Woodward did. The fact is though, I believe him.

....?

Why? What about the Aztec Club you young officers had in Mexico City --- now, that wasn't a prayer group, was it? I've heard that over a hundred dollars a day crossed the bar at the old Aztec. Even General Scott had to step in to be sure that you sports didn't get out of hand.

....

Oh, you say it was an exception, General. Sorry, Sir, I don't think so. What about Detroit --- your second assignment after Mexico?

....?

Hmm, you didn't think that I knew about Detroit. Well, I do know about it, including the story about the barrel of whiskey in the sutler's store --- always miraculously replenished--- and the tin cup which was constantly in use. You were no Son of Temperance in Detroit, were you?

... ...

No, I didn't think so.

Can we at least agree that you were no teetotaler when you were a lieutenant and a captain?

... .

Great, because it's time to take a look into your life on the Pacific Coast --- the place where drinking really got you into trouble.

....

Oh, sure, I remember how you loved the West and that you wanted to settle there some day.

... ...

Yes, General, I suppose that's true. It's the one thing you were cheated out of when Lincoln appointed you to Lieutenant-General. But let's not get off the subject. We're talking about the West Coast as it was in 1852, when you as a captain were making less money than a cook, when you couldn't afford to bring Julia and the family to join you, when your second child, Buck...

....!

Oh, excuse me, General, --- there I go with those nicknames again --- I meant Ulysses Jr. was born. You were still there when he celebrated his first birthday. You know, I'm surprised that you speak of it so well. It really wasn't a happy time for you.

....

Yes, you tried to supplement your income so you could bring Julia and the boys west. Shipping ice to San Francisco was a great idea --- if it hadn't melted before it got there, or the potato farm on the banks of the flooded Columbia River, and the other speculations you tried with Captains Waller and McConnell which never paid off.

....!

Oh, now you can laugh at them.

....

Yes, I have to agree with you that the chicken fiasco now seems funny. Sam Grant, trying to be the Colonel Sanders of California --- only to have them all die before they reached San Francisco.

....

Say, that's a good one, General, they certainly must have been "foul fowl" when they got there. But let's face it. You didn't think it was funny then.

Your housekeeper (surely you remember Mrs. Sheffield, don't you?) told of your true feelings. She said your eyes would fill with tears when you read Julia's letters and you would say, "Mrs. Sheffield, I have the dearest little wife in the world and I want to resign from the army and live with my family."

I'm sorry, General, I didn't want to upset you with sad memories, but we have to talk about the West Coast. It's the place where all this talk about Grant's drinking began. Now tell me, General, was Lloyd Lewis right when he wrote that "... living in such an atmosphere and honing as he was for Julia, the Son of Temperance gave up his fraternal vows..."

....

Heavens, no, sir, he didn't mean that you did nothing out there but hit the bottle --- and I don't think so either. Your old army friend, Lt. Henry Hodges, may have hit it about right when he said, "Sam was not by any means a drunkard, he merely went on two or three sprees a year --- and was always open to reason, and when spoken to on the subject would own up and promise to stop drinking, which he did." And your old West Point instructor, William Conant Church, discussed your drinking in his biography about you: "Grant had one physical weakness, and that was the incapacity to take the smallest drink of spirituous liquor without being overcome by it ... at rare intervals when a young officer, he would be betrayed into what was for him an overindulgence."
....

What was that? You say that everybody drank out there so you don't see why your little sprees should have caused such a stir. Well, you're right; unfortunately your high jinks crossed two people who were to have a real impact on your future --- George McClellan, and your boss, Lieutenant Colonel Robert Buchanan.
....

Pardon me, Sir? Why do I bring up McClellan? No, he wasn't all that important then. He too was only a captain. But he was an up and coming captain and he wasn't at all pleased when you went on one of your sprees when you were supposed to be outfitting his Northern Pacific Railroad survey team. But we'll get back to him later.

Buchanan was the real key to what happened to you out west. He had taken a personal dislike to you years before...
....

Yes, I understand that the disagreement came over some petty problem and that the feeling was mutual. Let's face it though, Captain Sam Grant's situation had just about hit rock bottom when Buchanan gave you the axe. If he hadn't been the one, another commander probably would have done the job.

....

Sure, there were plenty of reasons for you to hit the skids. You knew that you could be in that assignment forever and that you would never have enough money to bring Julia and the children to join you. It didn't help either that Julia was not a faithful correspondent. Many times you complained to her that it had been weeks or even months since you had received a letter. Moreover, your old friends were not with you at Fort Humboldt and your duties were little more than those of a clerk. It's no wonder that you wrote to Julia in early 1854, "I do nothing but set [sic] in my room and read and occasionally take a short ride on one of the public horses."

....

No, that was not at all like you --- the Sam Grant of the fast horse fame --- and it really wasn't your nature to sit alone. You may not have been rated as a great conversationalist (unless someone asked about the Mexican War, then it was "Away we go!"), but you were always part of the group, adding your two cents or wry wit to the banter once in a while. The fact is, you were becoming notorious for being a solitary and frequent drinker and ...

....

Oh, you say that you were just a "social drinker." Do you really believe that? Then explain to me how a social drinker guzzles straight whiskey from a tumbler filled to a measure of four fingers?

No, it was not merely a social drinker whom Colonel Buchanan took to task. "Resign or face charges," he said. You were soon heading home.

So was born the legend that "Grant drinks." As William Conant Church wrote:

... his difficulty with Buchanan affected him injuriously through the whole of his military career. The Army is as prone to gossip as a New England sewing society; and the stories of his experiences at Fort Humboldt were spread abroad in an exaggerated form, subjecting him to unjust suspicions and false charges that discredited him with his superiors, and aroused popular clamor against him at critical periods.

....

Yes, Sir, that was the beginning of the drinking stories, but what happened when you tried civilian life didn't help to slow the rumors down. First you lost the farm that Julia's father had given you, then the real estate partnership with Henry Boggs failed, finally, you missed out on the appointment as county engineer. You were close to hitting bottom again. To top it off, St. Louis was the crossroads of the Midwest, a place that your old army cronies were certain to pass through as they changed assignments. Can you blame them for jumping to conclusions? They had heard the tales from the West Coast and then they met a seedy loser in a faded blue overcoat who obviously couldn't make ends meet. What more did they need to be convinced that "Grant drank." The fact is, though, these rumors were not entirely true.

Do you remember your St. Louis neighbor, Judge Long?

....

That's right, the fellow who rode to town with you to sell wood. The Judge tried to set the record straight after the drinking rumors began again. He said that the stories started on one of your wood selling excursions when you came down with an attack of the ague --- today we'd probably call it influenza. The Judge claimed that a neighbor who saw you arrive home doubled over with chills and pain said, "Oh, your friend Grant came home drunk --- flat on his back -- yesterday." Judge Long stated that you hadn't had a drop of liquor all day, but "... the story thus started found such a swift wing that my denials and explanations never did overtake the lie. ... Grant, not only did not drink to excess, but seldom drank at all."

There's more evidence to support Judge Long's contention. Your Army buddy, Henry Coppeé, was quick to say that when you joined old friends you drank nothing but water, and several others who passed through St. Louis told the same story. Apparently, you had Julia and the children, and even though you were admittedly "solving the problem of poverty," the combination of loneliness and frustration which drove you to the bottle out west wasn't there. St. Louis may have been a financial disaster, but the descriptions of you roughhousing with your brood and your quips about your circumstances don't seem to paint the same picture of despair which were so evident at Fort Humboldt.

Now what do you have to say about the move to Galena and the job in your father's leather goods store?

....

I didn't think that job was to your liking; selling just wasn't your thing. But you're right, Galena may have been one of the most important moves you ever made. That's where you made the contacts   that pushed your military career literally to the stars.

.... ?

Exactly --- people like Congressman Elihu Washburne who helped you to get a regimental command and then badgered Lincoln to promote you to brigadier-general. Also John Rawlins, the lawyer and confirmed teetotaler, who was your chief of staff throughout the war.

....

Yes, Rawlins knew you in Galena, and this man who cursed "old demon rum" with a passion, and let the world know his feelings, spoke of your behavior in Galena. He said that while you smoked a clay pipe to excess, you were temperate in everything else and had totally abstained from drink for several years. Even the town bartender has been quoted as saying that when an Eastern salesman took you in for a drink, you always took a cigar instead.

Tell me, General, do your friends overstate the case? I mean is it true that you never took a drink after you left the Army?

....

I thought you did, but not with the same gusto as out west. I think that we can agree that you were in control of the situation.

....

No, no you don't. We aren't going to let it rest there. We have to see what happened when you were back in the Army and without Julia again.

... .!

You can call me whatever you like, General, but we're going to finish this. Now where were we --- you were back in the Army and wearing the stars of a brigadier-general, but a general without a command. Then the same good fortune which had suddenly opened up a regimental command for you back in Illinois and also had arranged the surprising promotion to brigadier was to smile on you again. General John Frémont, California's Old Pathfinder, was the commander in the West and he knew little about you --- and certainly nothing about your reputation in the old army. He intended to make you the District Commander of Southeast Missouri. Do you know how close you came to being put out to pasture before your new career had even begun?

....

I thought that you probably had some idea. Badeau was good at going through old records. Frémont's staff was quick to tell him what a mistake he was about to make. "Grant is unfit for command," they argued, "He drinks. He's the officer out west who had to resign because he couldn't leave the bottle alone."

Bruce Catton editorialized about this period of your career:
... the dark film left by gossip can never be entirely scrubbed away. In an army famous for hard drinking done by men in shoulder straps, this was the handicap Grant would always have to carry ... the stain deposited by gossip is still there, and men still cock their eyes and leer knowingly when Grant's name is mentioned: He drank.

For men who do not know him that has been enough.

....

True enough, Frémont may have done little right while he was the western commander, but he did ignore his babbling staff and let you have the command.

You really took command, too. Paducah (which first brought you to Lincoln's attention), Belmont, Fort Henry and finally, Fort Donelson. Suddenly, you were a national hero. You were "Unconditional Surrender" Grant --- but once again the rumors were flying and you were under a cloud. General Henry Halleck, who had replaced Frémont, was not pleased to have a drunkard receive the glory. He wired McClellan that he had reports that " ... you had resumed your former bad habits...." McClellan, remembering his earlier problems with your little sprees, was not the least surprised. He gave Halleck authority to arrest you --- and Halleck might have done it had it not been for Lincoln's intervention. So, Halleck, with his usual courage, let the matter drop, but then came the slaughter at Shiloh.

It's hard for even you to argue that the first day of the battle was not a disaster. Your army had been surprised and appeared to be on the brink of being pushed into the Tennessee River. You drove the Rebels on the second day, but that was too late to stop the gossip that you had been drunk. How else could you have been so completely surprised? Again Lincoln suppressed the agitators: "I can't spare this man; he fights." But even Lincoln began to lose faith as the Vicksburg Campaign dragged on through the winter of 1863. He was not only aware but was actually happy that Secretary of War Stanton was sending Charles Dana to Vicksburg to check on you.

....

Oh, yes, General, we know that you and your staff understood that Dana was a War Department spy and I'm happy to hear that you consider him to have been one of your most important wartime acquaintances. Nevertheless, he was at Vicksburg for one reason only --- to see if Grant imbibed heavily.

OK, General, what do you have to say about all this?

....

You don't know what I'm talking about? Come on now. You were well aware of the stories filtering back to Washington about you. You even brought them up in your *MEMOIRS*. You were being called a drunk, an incompetent ass, and even less polite epithets. Then Dana arrived. You *HAD* to know that you were on the spot again.

.... ?

Well, he proved to be a real friend. His first report to Washington squared things immediately. Dana's glowing dispatches, praising you for being industrious and sober, fully restored Lincoln's confidence in the fighting general he knew he couldn't spare.

... . ?

So, you want me to ask John Rawlins about you. Sure, he was with you through the entire war.

... .?

Certainly we know that Rawlins hated liquor with a passion, He had your staff so petrified they would not even mention liquor when he was within earshot. "Rawlins was death on liquor," they said. He even wrote to Congressman Washburne when the rumors about your drinking sprouted. "If you could only look into General Grant's countenance," he said, "You would want no other assurance of his sobriety."

....?

No, that's not all he said --- surely you remember that Rawlins was never at a loss for words. He went on: "Have no fears: Should General Grant at any time become an in-temperate man or an habitual drunkard, I will notify you immediately ... or resign my commission."

....?

Yes, I see your point. Rawlins stayed with you for the whole four years --- often chiding, frequently ranting, sometimes writing --- but he stayed.

....

I have to agree with you. I don't think Rawlins would have stayed if you had been a drunkard. What was that, General?

....

Oh, Admiral Foote. Yes, I know who you mean. He was the gunboat commander who was with you at Henry and Donelson.

....

How right you are. He was another "death on liquor" gentleman.

....

Is that so? He wouldn't even allow grog on his ships. That must have been cause for mutiny in those days. But as you say, you and he certainly seemed to get along well. Julia even included him among your "pleasant acquaintances" and he was one of your most vehement defenders when Halleck tried to destroy you after Donelson.

....?

That's what I said. Foote passed the word to Dana who in turn cleared the air with Stanton and Lincoln while Halleck and McClellan were haggling about what to do with you.

....

Yes, I would say that Foote was both your friend and admirer. So we have Rawlins and Foote, both of whom would have considered the Women's Christian Temperance Union intemperate, in your corner. An interesting twosome, and certainly not a pair who would have befriended nor tolerated a drunk as the commanding general.

Say, General, let me throw in one more. There was a lady who wrote a book after the war in which she talked about meeting you. Do you remember Mary Livermore and her Sanitary Commission group who visited you at Vicksburg?

....

Right! She was the commissioner who wanted several sick soldiers discharged from the Army. As she headed for Vicksburg she expected the worst about the condition of the army --- and Ulysses Grant. Now this lady had been around; in her own words she was one who "... had become practiced in the diagnosis of drunkenness." Based on this experience, though, she had concluded that: "Grant was not a drunkard, thank God! The clear eye and the steady nerves gave lie to the universal calumnies concerning his intemperate habits." That's quite a testimonial from a gal who, as she said, knew a drunk when she saw one.

You know, I think that we are getting someplace now. Look at the loyal friends you had. Charles Dana, Admiral Foote,

Admiral Porter, Sherman, McPherson, Old Stoneface Rawlins, and let's not forget Mary Livermore and her gang.

....

No it doesn't make sense to me that people of their stature would have remained loyal to you if you were in the habit of being poured into bed every night. General, there's one peculiar thing, have you noticed that all these drinking stories seemed to dry up after Lincoln pinned that third star on you?

....

Well, that's true. In late 1864, General "Baldy" Smith did claim that the reason you relieved him was that General Butler had gotten you stoned and was blackmailing you.

....

No. It doesn't hold water --- it wasn't long before you sent Butler packing too. Either the story is a phoney or Butler was the world's worst blackmailer.

It is still interesting, however, that your biographers hardly mention your "drinking habits" during the last year of the war.

....

Yes, General, that tells me something as well.

Well, General, we've covered a lot of territory and a good part of your life. Do you think that we have the whole story?

....

Good! I'm glad we can agree that you had your problems with the "old demon" at times, but it truly doesn't seem to have had the death grip on you that legend would have us believe.

....

Now, come on. Don't try to tell me that all of the stories were fairy tales. What about the boat trip to Satartia during the Vicksburg siege, for instance. Dana and Sylvanus Cadwallader, the newspaper man, were with you. (Even Julia had to comment on that trip when it became public after you had died). And let's not forget that Rawlins mentioned your staff's wild victory celebration after the fall of Vicksburg. So there *were* incidents, but the difference between these situations and what happened on the West Coast is that these were just that --- incidents. More importantly, none of them seem to have had any impact on your ability to command armies in battle.

Stephen Oates, in his biography of Lincoln, had some comments about you as well. I'd like to know how you feel about this description:

Grant may have had his troubles with the bottle in his early life but by the Civil War he seems to have imbibed no more than most army officers in that hard drinking time. He enjoyed a glass, and on rare occasion may have enjoyed one too many, but there is no documentary evidence that he was the chronic drunk his foes made him out to be. By now [1863] Lincoln had little interest in allegations about Grant's binges; the General conducted campaigns beyond the capacity of an inebriated lout.

... .

I agree, Sir, what satisfied Lincoln should be good enough for us too. Well, General, do you think that we've brought this drinking business into the open? Is there anything that you think we've left out?

....

Yes, I think that we've touched all the bases. Let me say that it's been very pleasant having this little chat with you. Until we get a chance to meet again, "Here's mud in your eye."

CHAPTER THREE

"PLEASE CALL ME BY THE ONLY NICKNAME I LIKE: GENERAL!"

From Hiram Ulysses to "Unconditional Surrender" Grant

SYNOPSIS: In this chapter we will flesh out the Prologue's thumbnail sketch of Grant's early life and take him through the triumph and tragedy of Fort Donelson. We will also meet many of the leading players in the opening phases of the Civil War.

There was Abraham Lincoln, of course, inaugurated in March of 1861 and Simon Cameron, Lincoln's first Secretary of War but quickly replaced by Edwin Stanton. The Army's Commander-in-Chief at the time of Fort Sumter was Brevet (or honorary) Lieutenant-General Winfield Scott. Scott, however, was seventy-five and in poor health (he had been a general in the War of 1812). Within a few months he retired and was succeeded by George Brinton McClellan, West Point class of 1846 and only thirty-five years old when the war began. "Little Napoleon" his admirers called him, and McClellan planned, in his *own* good time, to lead his *Army into Richmond* and bag the entire hostile government.

In the Western Theater, Major-General John Frémont --- California's "Pathfinder" and first senator, as well as the Republican Party's first candidate for President --- held sway with the airs of an imperial Caesar. Frémont eventually assumed the cloak of a Caesar, ran afoul of Lincoln and was replaced by Major-General Henry Halleck.

General Halleck was a devoted student of the campaigns of Napoleon and had earned the sobriquet "Old Brains" for his translation of Antoine Jomini's "Precis de l'art de la guerre" ---

*a study of Napoleon's campaigns and tactics. Sharing leader-
ship with him in the West was Brigadier-General Don Carlos
Buell, West Point '41. He had assumed the command of the
Department of the Ohio from the mentally unstable William
Tecumseh Sherman. This triumvirate --- McClellan, Halleck
and Buell --- believed that they were the last word on the strategy
to be used to conquer the Confederacy and through early 1862
they kept the Union telegraph wires humming as they discussed
their strategic concepts. Lincoln, the Cabinet, and the Congress,
however, wanted action, not words, but this group refused to be
pressed.*

*General William Sherman will make his appearance, as he,
like Grant, will begin his climb from the depths to the heights. In
addition, General C. F. Smith (West Point '25 and Commandant of Cadets there when Sherman and Grant were under-
graduates) will shoot across the western sky like a meteor only
to have his blazing light extinguished by an unfortunate accident.
Had he lived, the list of Civil War heroes may have been quite
different from that which we know. In the final analysis, however, it was on Grant that Lincoln focused. Grant's aggressive
moves at Paducah, Kentucky; Belmont, Missouri; and Forts
Henry and Donelson in Tennessee proved to the President that
he had one general who preferred fighting to talking and despite
the calumnies heaped upon Grant by his associates, the President staunchly supported him until the end of the war.*

Hello. General Grant, I'm happy to meet you for another of
our discussions.

....

No Sir, no alcohol talk today. Now that doesn't mean that
it won't come up. If drinking allegations have a bearing on our
discussions we'll mention it.

....

You noticed that too, General. It does seem that today's newspapers are full of stories about people in government with drinking problems --- or, I suppose, we should say alleged drinking problems. It's euphemistically called *substance abuse* now and considered a disease. That way they can use it as an excuse for malfeasance. I'm just glad that we have that discussion behind us.

....

I'll bet that you are, too.

....?

Today's topic? How about your early years? How you grew up, West Point, the War with Mexico, why you left the Army and your return to uniform. Then, if we have time, a little about the early months of the Civil War and we'll wind up with the battles at Forts Henry and Donelson. That should keep us busy, don't you think?

....

Yes, General, it is a full plate, but let's give it a try.

....

No, I'm not worried about you holding up your end of the conversation. Some historians describe you as "The Sphinx," but I've always thought that the description "quiet man" suited you better. We both know of too many instances when you were not hesitant in the least to throw some verbal fat into the fire.

....

If you want some examples, how about the fight with General Halleck after the Fort Donelson surrender. We'll be getting into the details of that post-battle battle in just a while. Another of your fights was with Secretary of War Stanton of all people. Remember early 1864? You were in Washington preparing for the great offensive and he challenged your authority to move troops away from Washington. "I rank the

Secretary in this matter," you argued, and forced Stanton to take the problem to the President. Even that didn't satisfy you. When Stanton asked you to state your case, you not so politely reminded him that it was because of him that the two of you were in the President's office and that, therefore, you had no case to make. "I am satisfied as it is," you needled. You may have been self-effacing and certainly gave the appearance of being modest, but you never were a meek or timid person.

....

That's right, Lincoln did take your part in the argument --- and we shouldn't forget your fight with President Johnson when he tried to indict General Lee for treason.

....

I know that you were furious. At Appomattox you gave your word that Lee could not be harassed by the Federal government as long as he honored his parole. Suddenly Lincoln's successor was saying that the word of U. S. Grant didn't count.

....

Yes. Johnson *did* finally back down, but what would you have done had he not?

....

You think that there may have been another rebellion. I doubt that you would have had to have gone that far. Your prestige was so high that President Johnson could not have stood up to you.

... .

Enough of this wandering, General, let's get on with your story.

You were born in 1822 and immediately there was trouble within the family over your name.

....

Oh! I'm sorry, Sir. I suppose I should tell them that Point Pleasant, Ohio was the place and April 27th, the date. But the point I want to make is that immediately there was trouble about your name.

....

No, it won't be the last time. In fact, it will take seventeen years and an act by Congress to resolve the problem officially and I doubt that your nicknames were ever really resolved...

....

Yes, Sir, I remember that you gave me your opinion on nicknames the other day, so we won't go into that again. But you should remember the family talking about how your father and mother took you to visit your mother's family for your christening. "Hiram will be his name," Grandfather Simpson said. "Ulysses is better!" Grandmother Simpson whispered demurely --- even she would not make a frontal assault against the old man. Jesse Grant, your father and always the family Solomon, solved the dilemma --- Hiram it would be with Ulysses the middle name: Hiram Ulysses Grant --- a fine name and a fine solution.

....

Yes, General, that's true. In the long run, Grandmother Simpson won. Your name may have been Hiram, but the family always called you Ulysses. Do you think that she planned it that way --- a flank attack when she knew a frontal assault would not win?

....

I'm surprised that you remember it all so clearly, and later you made it clear that you preferred Hiram. "Ulysses" gave you your first distaste for nicknames. The neighborhood children would taunt you with "Useless" and "Lyssus" and you insisted that your name was "Hiram." So it bounced back and forth until it came time for you to leave for West Point. Then you were sure that you would win and the name would be Hiram --- until you saw the initials H.U.G. on your luggage. HUG was not going to be your next nickname; or something even worse --- like "Huggy" or "Huggybear?"

....?

It doesn't take a genius to answer that one, General. The solution was to pry off the initials and go to the Point as Ulysses Hiram. There wasn't much they could do with "UHG," was there?

....

No, that wasn't the end of the story. As you say, your appointment, due to the sponsoring congressman's oversight, was reserved for Ulysses Simpson Grant and, with the government's typical love of red tape, only Ulysses Simpson Grant was going to be enrolled into West Point. If it had to be that way, you decided on the spot, so be it. You became U.S. Grant, Class of 1843 --- and the nickname game started again. First you became "United States" Grant, but that wouldn't do. Then, "Uncle Sam" --- better, but how about just "Sam." Perfect, and Sam became the only name your classmates ever used.

....

I must agree with you, General. Sam was better than Hug, but we both know that you would have preferred just Hiram.

At any rate, you were graduated from West Point in 1843 as a brevet second lieutenant. In 1845, you were with General Zachary Taylor near the Texas-Mexican border. Soon the war came and you saw your share of action: Palo Alto, Resaca de la Palma, Monterey, and then you joined General Winfield Scott for the drive from Vera Cruz to Mexico City.

....

What was that, General? Oh, I didn't realize that the only battle you missed in the entire war was Buena Vista.

....

I understand that that doesn't include California, but even so that really was quite a record. Not many of your classmates had the opportunity to see that much of the war and the two leading generals. You also had the chance to see many officers in battle who would later be wearing stars on both sides of the rebellion: Lee, Joseph E. Johnston, Albert Sidney Johnston, Pillow, and Pemberton, for instance, became Confederate generals; Meade, Buell, McClellan were a few who served the Union. Late in life you recalled your experiences with these officers and wrote:

The acquaintance thus formed was of immense service to me in the war of the rebellion --- I mean what I learned of the characters of those to whom I was afterward opposed. The natural disposition of most people is to clothe a commander of a large army, whom they do not know, with superhuman abilities. A large part of the National Army, for instance, and most of the the press of the country, clothed General Lee with just such qualities, but I had known him personally, and knew that he was mortal; and it was just as well that I felt this.

....

Oh certainly, General, we'll discuss these personalities more thoroughly as we go along. Pillow, Lee, A. S. Johnston, Bragg and Joe Johnston along with Pemberton faced you on the battlefield, so we'll be talking a lot more about each one.

As it happened, you returned from Mexico in 1848 and almost immediately married Julia Dent. You had a reasonably happy family life, one son and another baby on the way. Then your regiment was transferred to the West Coast. That was a terrifying trip, if you remember it.

.. ..

I guess that it would be almost impossible to forget --- most of your regiment, many with wives and children, were abandoned in the jungles of Panama by an unscrupulous transportation contractor. How many of the group died before you reached the Pacific coast?

....

One hundred? My, God! That was about one quarter of the total and almost all from cholera. Let's face it, though. Had it not been for your resourcefulness in getting a new contract for pack mules, the entire company may have perished. Once again you demonstrated your ability to master predicaments and after a very difficult six weeks the survivors were sailing north to San Francisco.

....

This time I agree, General. We've already said enough about your problems in the Oregon territory, so let's move right ahead to 1854 --- the year you resigned from the Army. I think that after ten years in the service you were truly disappointed about leaving. After all you had just been promoted to permanent captain and....

....

Of course you were anxious to get home to your family. Ulysses Jr. was two years old and you had never seen him, but I still think you had mixed emotions which you covered with a little bravado in front of your friends: "Whoever hears of me in ten years will hear of a well-to-do Missouri farmer," was your boast.

.... ?

Yes, Sir, we've all heard about your boast and, with the sixty acres Julia's father carved from his estate for you, your brave front might have been justified --- if you had known how to farm. You named it "Hardscrabble," and that's exactly what it was. Within four years the farm had failed and you were into a contrived real estate partnership with Julia's cousin, Harry Boggs. You were no more a salesman than you were a farmer and soon *Boggs & Grant* was dissolved. Then, after you were unable to wrangle a job as a St. Louis city engineer, it fell to your father to give you a job in his Galena, Illinois leather shop.

....

I know you were thankful that it wasn't old Jesse's tannery. You could still remember how that place made you retch when you were a boy. No, it was the leather shop, but that didn't change your situation. There you were, out of the Army for six years, 38 years old, a wife, four children, and dependent on your father for what amounted to an $800 a year handout. No wonder people who saw you scoffed at the man who was supposed to have been the "well-to-do" farmer and, in their gossipy way, muttered that " ... you really had no prospects at all."

You know, we've hinted some about your father and his idiosyncracies --- later we should be sure to talk about him and his peculiar ways. He gave you a hard time as a youth, packed you off to West Point because it was "thrifty," and very likely because he thought that you were better off in the military than in the business world.

....

No, he didn't say so outright, but he did say that he couldn't afford to lose any more money on your horse deals. That's a fairly good clue, wouldn't you say?

....

Perhaps I'm being somewhat harsh about it, General, but that's the way things were when you moved to Galena in 1860. I might have overstated the extent of your poverty --- not the financial poverty, that was all too true. But you were scraping by and anyone who examines your family life back then sees that it had its prosperous side.

I particularly like the story of your evening ritual with the children. As you climbed the long staircase to your house three year old Jesse would shout, "Mister, do you want to fight?" Your reply was always the same, "I'm a man of peace, but I'll not be hectored by a person of your size." Then the lilliputian donnybrook would begin with your brood eventually announcing triumph over the best battler in the world. How did they get that idea, anyway?

....

Oh, their uncles convinced them that you had won the Mexican War single-handedly --- and you, it seems, let them continue to believe it. You must have liked being a hero in their eyes.

The end of this idyllic scene, however, was fast approaching. Lincoln's election in November, 1860, had brought on the tidal wave of secession and with his inauguration came the flood of war. When Fort Sumter was fired upon and Lincoln called for 75,000 volunteers, you knew that West Pointers would be in great demand. After all, the armies which Taylor and Scott commanded in Mexico were just good sized divisions when compared to an army of 75,000. Seasoned officers would be desperately needed to mold a disciplined army out of such motley volunteers, both to train them and to lead them in battle.

....

Of course as a West Pointer you should have expected a regimental command. As you say, politicians with no military experience were wearing "instant" stars on their shoulders and true jokers were filling the ranks between lieutenant and colonel. That's why you can't be faulted for refusing the command of the company of Galena recruits, but...

....

That's what I was just going to say, General. For a while it looked as though you were being so picky that you were going to miss the war altogether --- that regimental command just never seemed to materialize.

....

True enough, Sir, the Lord often works in mysterious ways. While you were waiting, and almost at the point of despair, you did make what today we call "contacts." The most important was Elihu Washburne, the Federal Congressman from Galena and your fellow recruiting officer in Illinois. A Republican, he was closely connected to the President ....

....

Is that right? --- Washburne was the only government official to meet Lincoln at the depot when he arrived in Washington for his inauguration.

You also came in contact with Governor Yates of Illinois. You didn't know it then, but these two, Washburne and Yates, would eventually start you on your way to the top.

Something else that wasn't apparent to you at the time: It was a stroke of luck that you couldn't wrangle an appointment in you native Ohio. You thought that your former West Point and the old army colleague, George McClellan, would surely help. The newly commissioned Major-General of Ohio Volunteers pretended that you simply didn't exist when you visited his office.

....

General, they may be hard words, but you were having a very difficult time and I don't know any other way to say it. Look at your own comment about McClellan: "I called on two successive days at his office but failed to see him on either occasion ...." And even that doesn't tell the whole story; you then told of how you sat for hours watching his staff being "...

busy with quills ...." There's no doubt that you were hurt by "Little Napoleon's" cavalier attitude. You had known him at West Point, Mexico, and on the West Coast. In your *MEMOIRS* you still seemed to be rankled: "I was older," you wrote, "had ranked him in the Army, and could not hang around his headquarters watching the men with the quills ...." Don't you think that it was most fortunate that you never did get mixed up with McClellan? In the East your light never would have come out from under the barrel --- you *still* would be Colonel Grant.

....

I never saw such a smug look on you, General, but that's with the help of hindsight. In truth, at the time you were stunned and chagrined. If not Ohio or Illinois, then what? You tried Indiana where your classmate Joe Reynolds was a new colonel and had some influence with Governor Morton. Again, you were too late. An attempt to get command of a Missouri regiment and a direct request to the Federal Government both drew blanks. It was the repeated failures of St. Louis all over again.

....

Who could disagree with you, General? You had every reason to feel more depressed than ever before as you headed back from Ohio. How could this be? Neither Ohio, Missouri, Illinois, Indiana nor the Federal government had a place for you. Despite West Point, despite twelve years commissioned service, despite the fact that clowns were being made colonels and generals, professional soldier Ulysses -- or Hiram -- or Sam -- or whatever -- Grant was about to spend the war in a leather store in Galena. But there was one more roll of the dice coming before the game was over. This was the roll which would propel you into the White House.

While you were lobbying in Ohio, in June of 1861, Illinois' Governor Yates encountered a situation which desperately cried for an experienced military man. He needed someone to take command of a renegade volunteer regiment. "Governor Yates' Hellions," the locals had taken to calling the unruly bunch --- not the sort of public relations an elected official appreciates.

....

You're quite right. You do owe Governor Yates a thank you. But don't forget that it was your own efficient efforts in getting those Illinois recruits mustered which impressed him. Did you know that you were an absolute enigma to him?

....

No? That surprises me. I thought that someone who had been in Springfield that fateful spring would have mentioned the Governor's bewilderment. Look at it from his point of view. Here you were, a West Pointer who had been asked several times to stand for *election* to a regimental command, but on each occasion had adamantly refused. The governor was further confused because you gave him every indication that you wanted to serve the Union. Then someone explained to him that you had been Regular Army and in the Regulars officers were not *elected* to positions of responsibility. Once he understood your idiosyncrasy, he was quick to act --- and you were the colonel of the Seventh District Volunteer Regiment.

....

So, you recall the assignment as a mixed blessing because your regiment consisted of thirty-day volunteers whose enlistments were about to expire. You had a week to convince them to reenlist or it would have been back to Springfield to fill out more forms. Then John Logan and John McClernand, both noted politicians from Illinois and who later would be generals under your command, gave "Rally Round the Flag" speeches while you provided the leadership the men needed, and the inspired troops reenlisted almost to a man. Colonel Grant had a government job with a future. And that was just the beginning of your lucky streak.

....

All right, if you don't care for the word luck we can use something else --- call if "fortuitous circumstances" if you will, but no matter what name you give it, from the time you started your regiment marching to Missouri everything broke exactly right for you. Not only right, but in what may have been the only sequence which could have resulted in your wearing four stars.

....

What do you mean that good things come in bunches, General?

....

Really? You had no sooner agreed to Governor Yates's offer than you received word that Ohio also had a regiment for you. Think that you made the right choice?

....

Of course I was joking, but I agree, it's time to get on to Missouri and your first assignment with what was then called the 21st Illinois. You drilled the troops, made soldiers out of them and marched them after imaginary Rebels. They wore out shoe leather but accomplished little else. However, there was one minor incident which may have had a significant impact on *your* development as a battle commander. At least you must have thought that this occurrence was important because you relate every detail of it in your *MEMOIRS.*

....

That's the one all right --- the order you received to scatter Colonel Thomas Harris's rebel raiders. Why don't you describe it for us?

I received orders to move against Colonel Thomas Harris. ... While preparations for the move were going on I felt quite comfortable; but when we got on the road and found every house deserted I was anything but easy.... We halted at night on the road and proceeded the next morning at an early hour. Harris had been encamped in a creek bottom for the sake of being near water. The hills on either side of the creek extend to a considerable height, possibly more than a hundred feet. As we approached the brow of the hill from which it was expected we could see Harris' camp ... my heart kept getting higher and higher until it felt to me as though it was in my throat. I would have given anything then to have been back in Illinois, but I had not the moral courage to halt and consider what to do; I kept right on ... the marks of a recent encampment were plainly visible, but the troops were gone. My heart resumed its place. It occurred to me at once that Harris had been as much afraid of me as I had been of him. This was a view of the question I had never taken before; but it was one I never forgot afterwards. From that event to the close of the war. I never experienced trepidation upon confronting an enemy, though I always felt more or less anxiety. I never forgot that he had as much reason to fear my forces as I had his. The lesson was valuable.

Yes, General, the lesson was valuable, but it was only lesson number one in what may be a never-ending course. You still had to meet an enemy who stood up to you and was not forty miles away when you reached the battlefield, but that would come. For now let us say that the education you received in meeting the phantom Colonel Harris may have made this incident in Missouri one of the most important non-battles in the annals of the United States.

In the turmoil of 1861, mysterious things continued to happen. Less than two months after Governor Yates commissioned you a colonel (you hadn't even received the formal paperwork yet) you were selected to be a brigadier-general. ....

So, this was the work of Congressman Washburne whom you had impressed when you chaired the recruiting committee back in Galena. He was entitled to nominate a brigadier and you were the only qualified person he knew. He nominated, Lincoln signed, Congress approved, and you were soon wearing stars. An incredible run of luck? It certainly was, but this was only the beginning. ....

All right, let's get back to Missouri and the new brigadier-general. As I said, everything began to break exactly right. John C. Frémont was the senior Union officer in the West. He had been California's first senator and then the Republican party's first presidential candidate in 1856 --- a seemingly perfect selection for a high military command, but in reality he was woefully arrogant and inefficient. ....

I know you weren't a Frémont man in politics. You had voted for James Buchanan in '56, but now your future depended on how Frémont accepted you as one of his general officers. ....

Yes, Sir, there certainly was some question as to what assignment he would give you. He knew little about you, but as the ranking brigadier in the area he intended to make you a district commander. His staff, however, wasn't as sanguine as he about your getting the job. These were old army clods who immediately rushed to tell him that his new brigadier wouldn't do: "He drinks."

....

General, we *do* have to bring this up again and we now know that it was a lurking shadow throughout your career. Your future was hanging by a slender thread over this drinking business. Frémont was being told that, brigadier-general or not, he should get rid of you. The old maid coffee klatch mentality which afflicted these ersatz Puritans was probably the same disease which infected McClellan when he wouldn't see you and Lorenzo Thomas who never answered your letter to Washington. But Frémont was not part of the inner circle --- he didn't care what had happened ten years before. It must have helped, though, that you had one defender in the inner sanctum: Major Justus McKinstry, an old Regular Army man who saw something in you which the biddies refused to see. He defended you staunchly before Frémont and when the storm had settled, you were the commander of the Southwest Missouri District. Established in your new headquarters at Cairo, Illinois, you studied the military situation around southern Illinois and prepared to move on the key Kentucky river town of Paducah.

....

Certainly the move was a sound military decision. I've already said that Paducah was a key river town, but the way you did it was typically Grant. You were too army-wise to be insubordinate or to exceed your authority, so you simply telegraphed to Frémont what you intended to do: "Unless I hear from you to the contrary."

....

Yes, Sir, it was very military and very correct --- but what about the notice about moving "tonight." The most efficient headquarters would have been unable to meet your deadline for an answer --- with Frémont's haphazard organization, it was impossible.

....

So you knew it. Fortunately, it didn't matter, did it? When you had returned from Paducah, Frémont's approval was waiting for you. But Frémont was no longer an issue. A proclamation he had issued in Missouri (he forgot that he was a major-general, not the President) in which he threatened citizens and potentially emancipated the slaves, pushed Lincoln to relieve him. You were more fortunate. Almost simultaneously Lincoln read your eminently sensible proclamation to the citizens of Paducah. He was impressed, particularly with the part which read: "I have nothing to do with opinions. I deal only with armed rebellion and its aiders and abettors. You can pursue your usual avocations without fear or hindrance ...." The President is reported to have said, "The man who can write like that is fitted to command in the West."

....

Oh, it was a nice compliment all right, but surely based more on his pique at Frémont than admiration for an obscure brigadier. However, it's true that U. S. Grant was no longer an unknown to Lincoln -- a point which will be important in the political aftermath of the forthcoming conquest of Fort Donelson.

....

You are certainly right, Sir. Had Lincoln followed up on that remark and given you command in the West, he may have destroyed you. Army politics would have certainly worked against you and, just as importantly, you were not yet ready for high command. The time spent serving Halleck proved to be a useful primer for you in the handling of troops in battle, developing strategic concepts, and building your own confidence in the face of the enemy. I've often wondered if "confidence" was what your Battle of Belmont was all about.

....

I know that Belmont was only a "demonstration." It's purpose was to keep the enemy uncertain while Union forces maneuvered in Missouri, but you turned it into a pitched battle. In fact your men suffered over four-hundred casualties, and you later said of it: "The National troops acquired a confidence in themselves at Belmont that did not desert them through the war." Many people have argued that U. S. Grant needed the confidence builder more than the troops did. After all, you admitted to feeling anxious as you marched toward Harris; it's only logical that from then on you were looking for a chance to prove that you could effectively lead troops in battle.

....

Of course you knew that you had courage. You had proved that in Mexico. What may have concerned you was not the raw courage of a trooper, but maintaining the ability to function as a battle commander. As the Civil War continued, some very respectable commanders, such as Joe Hooker and John Pope, would drift into a blue funk when they donned the mantle of ultimate responsibility.

....

That's exactly what I mean. You expected General Pillow to freeze when you made your move on Donelson. You had seen him operate in Mexico and felt quite certain about him, didn't you?

....

It has everything to do with it, General. In autumn of 1861, you did not know that you wouldn't suffer from the same loss of nerve syndrome that you had seen affect other generals.

....

Your argument is very convincing and heart touching, General, but I still see an ulterior motive behind such a strong "demonstration." Look at the record. You know it better than anyone, no matter how much you may try to gloss over certain parts of it: You were thirty-nine years old and had hardly done a thing right in your life. Your father continually ragged you about both your lack of any sense for business and for letting your West Point education addle you further; now you had the opportunity to prove him wrong. In the deepest regions of your own heart and soul you believed that the firstborn son of Jesse Grant *could* lead a regiment, or a brigade, or a corps. You believed that U.S. Grant could lead an *army* and, if called upon, he could lead *THE ARMIES*. But the movement against Colonel Harris had drummed up just a little shadow of doubt within you --- after Belmont no more shadows.

Another thing I want to ask about the battle. Many of us have never understood your remark about Belmont giving the National troops confidence. Fewer than thirty-five hundred men accompanied you to Belmont. To say that a single brigade's experience forged the mettle for the western armies seems to be pushing your rationalization just a little too far. I still say that Belmont was really a part of the military education of U.S. Grant.

....

Well, General, on that we'll have to agree to disagree. We're probably two old nuts too petrified to be cracked. The other part of Belmont which has been a matter of never ending controversy is the matter of which side won.

....

I know that you claimed victory and what you say is generally true. Your "demonstration" did allow the other Union forces to maneuver without interference from the Confederate forces in the Belmont-Columbus area. But even after the Union soldiers' initial success on the battlefield, the reinforced enemy drove your men back to their transports. If the battle was a raid or demonstration then you accomplished your purpose and you can claim victory. If it was a battle, then you lost.

....

I suppose that you're right. It was a battle in which there were no losers --- unless, as I believe, it was a fight to prove that Jesse Grant's son could lead troops in a fight; then the North had a big win. It just seems that after Belmont your light finally did come out from under the barrel and long-range plans began forming --- the plans for riverine warfare which you had mentioned to Colonel Emerson back in Missouri were taking shape. An invasion of the Southland was about to become a reality.

....

That's the truth, Sir. Getting General Halleck to think offensively was more of a job that whipping the Rebels. Remember? There were three geniuses in the Army: McClellan in Washington, Buell in Kentucky (in the job which had driven Sherman to a "rest-home" assignment), and Halleck in St. Louis. They exchanged wires on offensive strategy and convinced each other that it was impossible to launch an offensive despite the pleadings of the President. What was it you said, General, about your timid colleagues?

....

That's the one, Sir, the comment about Napoleon, let's hear it:

Some of our generals failed because they worked out everything by rule. They know what Frederick the Great did at one place, and Napoleon at another. They were always thinking about what Napoleon would do. Unfortunately for their plans, the rebels would be thinking about something else. I don't underrate the value of military knowledge, but if men make war in slavish observance of the rules, they will fail.... Consequently, while our generals were working out problems ... that would have looked well on a blackboard, practical facts were neglected. To that extent I consider remembrances of old campaigns a disadvantage.... . War is progressive, because all the instruments of war and its elements are progressive.... .

That sums up what was going on in 1861 --- very little. Then in early 1862 you exploded onto the national scene with victories at Fort Henry and Fort Donelson.

....

I suppose that I do make it sound too easy. Your first attempt to get Halleck's approval met with outright failure. In your own words, "I was cut short as if my plan was preposterous."

....

You may be very right, Sir. Had it not been for Admiral Foote's encouragement and intervention with Halleck, Donelson may still be in Rebel hands. A few days after your meeting with Halleck, the aggressive Foote (Do I smell a conspiracy?) wired his own proposal to move on Fort Henry. Double teamed and confident that Foote could accomplish what *he* had outlined, Halleck suddenly saw the proposal as an opportunity for his command to meet the President's call for action. He envisioned himself becoming the number two man in the Army with overall command in the West; he relented and approved the Fort Henry mission.

....

What you're saying was quite true --- as a military installation Fort Henry was a joke --- a travesty of military construction. In fact, you and Foote moved South in late January, but before you could even get your troops into position to attack,

Foote's gunboats had blasted the Tennessee River forts into submission.

You thought that capturing Henry and Hieman, its companion fort, had been such a simple operation, why stop? After all, you saw the havoc that the Navy had wreaked --- obviously the Navy's gunboats were invincible against such structures.

....

Oh, you were convinced all right. Your victory wire to Halleck told the story: "Fort Henry is ours. The gunboats silenced the batteries before the investment was completed. ... ." Then came the tip-off to your presumptuous thinking. "I shall take and destroy Fort Donelson on the 8th and return to Fort Henry." The 8th was just one day after the fall of Fort Henry --- now that's confidence. March to a position a half a day away, defeat the enemy, occupy the fort, and return to Henry the next day. A good idea, Sir, but you were wrong. Fort Donelson was the far stronger installation; a fact that no one --- not you, not Halleck, not Foote, not even the Confederate regional commander, General A. S. Johnston --- really understood. After the debacle at Henry, Johnston wired Richmond: "I think the gunboats of the enemy will probably take Fort Donelson without the necessity of employing their land force in cooperation."

....

Reconsider? I'll bet that you soon wanted to reconsider. Look at your later comment: "Then, too, it would not have been prudent to proceed without the gunboats." Your staff ride to Donelson quickly proved that this was no Fort Henry --- it was a formidable piece of military engineering. Nevertheless, you had to make your move soon. The question was: How to get General Halleck's approval?

Once again, you really didn't get your superior's approval for the operation --- it was a repeat of Paducah. Halleck would have to order you *NOT* to march on Donelson. There was a purpose in your playing games with Halleck: Your force was actually smaller than the army in the fort, something which was absolutely against the rules of warfare. You knew that a direct request would never have sold.

....

As you say, you had some advantages which you didn't think would carry much weight with Halleck. General Floyd, who was in command, you knew was no soldier, and, as you later wrote, "I judged that he would yield to Pillow's pretension." You had known Pillow in Mexico and had seen that he lacked daring in combat. He, you felt, would allow you to march right to the base of his defenses without a move against you and on this slim reed you bet your entire command.

....

So, despite the rules, you believed that "... 15,000 men on the 8th of February would be more effective that 50,000 a month later." As it happened, you took your fifteen thousand and invested a fort which housed almost twenty-one thousand when the rules dictated that you should have had closer to one hundred thousand. No wonder you were anxious for the gunboats to arrive at Donelson before Halleck could figure out exactly what was happening between the rivers.

....

That's right, I hadn't considered that. This *was* the beginning of the Army of the Tennessee --- which became the most success-oriented Union army. From Donelson, its soldiers would march through the bloody fields of Shiloh, to the glory of Vicksburg, the rescue at Chattanooga, and, with Sherman, to Atlanta, Savannah and into North Carolina. Legends must begin someplace, and this Army's legend was about to begin on the banks of the Cumberland River at a place called Fort Donelson.

....

That's also a very important point, General. Donelson began the partnership of "Grant & Sherman" which may have been of more significance that the capture of the fort itself. Let's talk about the renewal of your acquaintance with Sherman a little later. Meanwhile, you were having a devil of a time with Fort Donelson.

....

All right, I'll concede that at first everything was going according to plan. You had marched your troops right to the door of the fort, the gunboats eventually puffed and paddled their way down the Tennessee and up the Cumberland Rivers. It seemed that the scene was set for an easy victory: "The plan was for the troops to hold the enemy within his lines, while the gunboats should attack the water batteries at close quarters and silence the guns if possible." The truth was that the gunboats took a terrible pounding from the heavy and well situated guns within Donelson. "... I only witnessed the falling back of our gunboats," you wrote later, "and felt sad enough at the time over the repulse ... The sun went down on the night of the 14th of February, 1862, leaving the army confronting Fort Donelson anything but comforted over the prospects." This is about as despondent as you were ever to become at any time during the war. Even after the first terrible day at Shiloh you were talking about whipping the enemy in the morning.

....

You really felt at that moment that the worst was yet to come. You had little desire to set up a formal siege when your men were not equipped for a long winter campaign. Could it have been that General Grant was not prepared for a long battle? You had optimistically told Halleck that you would take Donelson on the 8th --- now it was the 14th and you couldn't report victory yet. How much patience would Halleck have? You could see his options hovering over you like a vulture. He could either tell you to withdraw to Fort Henry (as his original order had directed), or, more likely, appoint a general he felt more comfortable with to direct the siege. Either way, U.S. Grant would have joined the other military has-beens who already were littering the countryside.

....

As you say, General, you had bet against Pillow and eventually he made the wager pay off. But not until he had shaken your troops out of their boots.

....

I'll bet you that you remember it well. While you were upriver conferring with the wounded Admiral Foote, Pillow attacked and actually crushed McClernand's division. He had surprised you by initiating an offensive action ("I had no idea that there would be any engagement on land unless I brought it on myself," you later said), but then he restored your faith in your ability to judge other generals. With either victory or escape just an inch away, incredibly Pillow called his men back into their trenches.

Thanks to Pillow's lack of intestinal fortitude, you were able to restore your right flank; direct General C. F. Smith to assault with your left wing; convince the quivering Floyd and Pillow to scurry away in the night; tell General Simon Bolivar Buckner that your terms were unconditional surrender; and then accept his surrender in a more congenial spirit.

....

I remember, Buckner was an old friend of yours. I believe that he had helped you with some money when you were sailing home from the West Coast in 1854. You always claimed that had he, and not Pillow, been in charge you would not have so cavalierly marched to the gates of Donelson. But Pillow had been in charge, you had known him in Mexico, and as you had anticipated, he had let you move into position unmolested. As a result you became "Unconditional Surrender" Grant, possibly the most celebrated general in the Union Army.

....

General, I have to disagree with you --- the battle did make you famous. This was the first meaningful Union victory and it came while McClellan was still "organizing" his Army of the Potomac, a full seven months after the disastrous battle at Bull Run.

If you *weren't* famous why did thousands of citizens send you cases of cigars after they had read that you fought the battle with a cigar stub clenched in your teeth.

....

The cigar may have been a courtesy proffered by Foote --- I know that you had always smoked a clay pipe --- but henceforth you began your day with a score of cigars in your pocket and even at that, in heated situations, you were forced to restock.

....

I knew that you would say that. There was always a "thrrrrrif-ty" side to you --- you were not going to let good cigars go to waste. I'd say a little of Jesse Grant had rubbed off on you. I also seem to remember a story that after Lee's surrender you were most anxious to get back to Washington to begin the dismantling of that huge military machine which was costing the government over $3,000,000 a day. But here we are getting ahead of ourselves again. Thrifty or not, you were being hailed as "*U.S. means Unconditional Surrender*" Grant.

....

That's right, Sir, another of those hateful nicknames; but even you have to admit that it did not chafe you as much as those when you were younger. "Unconditional Surrender" was applause from a grateful nation. It was a flag of vindication being waved at those who once had no faith in you: To Jesse Grant who ridiculed your business acumen, to father-in-law Dent who regarded you as a ne'er-do-well, to Buchanan who had drummed you out of the army, and to all of those lordly citizens of St Louis who regarded you with disdain. But the bubble you were riding didn't last and when it burst you were made to suffer the pangs of St. Louis and Galena all over again.

....

I recall that. Sir. After the war you found out the true story when your staff had access to the War Department files. The problem was with Halleck, McClellan, and Buell --- all the old boy members of the "What would Napoleon do?" club. They could neither understand nor admit that a nonmember of their club could achieve anything. Halleck, the records showed, was the worst of them. He asserted that the credit for the victory belonged to C. F. Smith and he urged that Smith be promoted to major-general. If Lincoln insisted on your promotion, then he wanted yours, Smith's, Buell's and John Pope's all to be coincident.

....

No doubt he *did* hope that when comparisons were made the administration would see its folly and let the leather clerk from Galena slip through the crack, or, at the very least, allow you to be buried in the sudden rush of major-generals.

....

Oh, sure! You always gave General Smith much of the credit for your early successes --- and Sherman agreed with you. I don't know of anyone who didn't believe that this salty old soldier, who was Commandant of Cadets at West Point when both you and Sherman were collecting demerits, was an extraordinary leader. Unfortunately, he had that political problem early in the war which delayed his promotion to general, then, just a few months after Donelson, he died from that leg infection. As you say, we'll never know what he might have achieved had he lived through the war.

....?

Yes, General, I do know what Sherman once said of him. Even though Sherman considered himself your friend and deeply admired your accomplishments, Sherman commented: "Had C. F. Smith lived, Grant would have disappeared into history after Fort Donelson." Your friend Sherman simply believed that, except for the injury to Smith, Halleck would have found some way around letting you resume command of the Army of the Tennessee.

You're not alone in agreeing with Sherman; you now know that Halleck truly disliked you and it was he, not McClellan, who was the primary instigator of the sea of troubles which seemed about to engulf you after Donelson. But I wonder. What you seem to overlook is that you were no longer the passive Sam Grant of Galena, you were now Unconditional Surrender Grant of Fort Donelson and that may have made a difference.

... .

Sorry, Sir, no more nicknames --- I was just trying to make a point. Now, what I was about to say was that if Halleck, McClellan, and the other "Napoleon Club" generals were going to end the rise of U. S. Grant, then they would have to do it over the raving objections of one Abraham Lincoln. I don't believe that Shiloh was needed to awaken Lincoln to the fact that he had one general in the whole United States

Army who, if given the opportunity, would fight. I think that what happened after Donelson shows this clearly.

You saw opportunity in the West while the "Napoleons" were seeing their personal glory trains derailed. You wanted to get on to Nashville which the Confederacy had abandoned after the fall of Donelson; you wanted to get to Corinth, the Mississippi railroad center; you wanted to get on to Vicksburg which at that time was virtually undefended. This conquest of the West would have been stupendous, they recognized, except that it was being planned by the wrong man. To them it was inconceivable that the conquering army should be led by a sloppy general who not only did not conduct his battles by the book...

....

Good point, General, it *WAS* Halleck's book. That's why they called Halleck "Old Brains," and he was annoyed when you ignored the rules which were in *his* book. But then he became infuriated when he was told that you simply didn't know anything about the book.

At any rate, that series of wires, which you later found, hummed to McClellan in Washington: "I have had no communication with General Grant for more that a week. He left his command without my authority and went to Nashville," (As you said, you had wired for approval to go to Nashville, but, typically, left before Halleck's answer arrived. As it happened, Halleck never received your wire). "His army seems to be as much demoralized by the victory of Fort Donelson as was that of the Potomac by the defeat of Bull Run. ... I am worn out and tired with this neglect and inefficiency. C. F. Smith is almost the only officer equal to the emergency." As we discussed earlier, he sent a second dispatch soon thereafter: "A rumor has just reached me that since the taking of Fort Donelson, General Grant has resumed his former bad habits. I ... have placed General Smith in command of the expedition up the Tennessee."

Halleck must have believed himself on solid ground. He had recently received a message from McClellan which gave him permission to arrest you and to place C. F. Smith in command. Then, Halleck made a tactical error.

............?

Yes, I do mean the wire to you: "You will place Major-General C. F. Smith in command of the expedition and remain yourself at Fort Henry, Why do you not obey my orders to report strength and positions of your command?"

....

Now we *all* know that this was the first you had heard of these orders and requests from Halleck --- a disloyal telegraph operator had disappeared with his headquarters' telegrams. But this was a new Grant. Halleck may have resembled the taunting images of Colonel Buchanan or an arm waving Jesse Grant; however, you were not about to be a silent penitent this time. You fired back that you had kept his headquarters informed --- if they had not considered the messages of sufficient importance to show to Halleck, why blame you? You assertively suggested that the game of innuendo be stopped. If Halleck felt that you had done something wrong it was time to press charges --- just stop this petty campaign of a thousand cuts. Then came the clincher from Washington, where Lincoln had been watching the entire game. The War Department suddenly asked for full details of your dereliction of duty and what Halleck intended to do about it.

....

It certainly had gotten out of hand. It was far beyond the bounds the "Napoleon Club" members had intended. Halleck decided to back down and advised you to report to Pittsburg Landing and resume command. "The power is in your hands;

use it, & you will be sustained by all above you," a chastened Halleck wrote to you.

....

The end result may have been proper and fitting; but that doesn't mean that it wasn't a traumatic experience for you. Through the entire proceedings one of those scourging migraine headaches, which always appeared when you were under extreme stress, plagued you with a vengeance. You wrote to Foote that it "... nearly destroys my energy." But you were back in command and the pain from the headache was gone.

....

So true, General. You were barely free of one situation when you became embroiled in an even greater pressure cooker --- the slaughter at Shiloh. Let's look at what was developing in that arena. For one thing, it brought you and Sherman together for the first time.

....

Yes, we know that you had worked with him during the investment at Fort Donelson. I meant that now you were in the same command --- a somewhat difficult situation for you both, wasn't it?

....?

Well, I say that because even though he had outranked you as a brigadier-general, he willingly supported your forces at Donelson and announced that if he had to come to Donelson he would have waived rank in order to let you continue in command. Such altruism was a rarity in the Civil War army. As a result of Donelson you were now a major-general and an army commander; Sherman was your subordinate and commanding a division. Despite this reversal in fortunes, there is no evidence that Sherman resented or objected to his status.

....

That's what I thought you would say, General. He was a remarkable man and friend. I think we should say a bit about him before we get involved in the killing fields of Shiloh.

You and Sherman had a lot in common. You knew him at West Point....

....

I understand, General --- he was a first classman when you were a plebe so you knew him only slightly at the Academy and even in the old army you had no more that a passing acquaintance. He too had resigned from the army and had had his troubles making his way as a civilian. You encountered him once while you were struggling in St. Louis, just after he had seen his banking business fail. "Banking and gambling are synonymous," he had written to his brother, and to you he commented that "West Point and the Regular Army aren't good schools for farmers, bankers, merchants and mechanics." He finally did have some success in providing for his family as he became the president of a college in Louisiana and later the president of the St. Louis street railway system.

When the war came, he was quick to volunteer. While you were working in the recruiting office in Illinois, Sherman was in service as a colonel and in August 1861, he was one of a group of Ohio colonels promoted to brigadier.

....

I think that you're quite right; he had fought at Bull Run and somehow the experience depressed him severely and the condition worsened when he was then sent to supervise activities along the Ohio-Indiana-Kentucky border. As you said, it was then that his psychological depression deepened and threatened to overwhelm him. He declared to anyone who would listen that hundreds of thousands of Rebels were opposing him and he insisted that he needed a force of at least two hundred thousand to guard his area. The newspaper

reporters covering his command dismissed Sherman's rant-
ings as those of an insane man, and many of his military
colleagues agreed. Sherman's hysteria finally resulted in his
being transferred to a quiet post in Missouri --- I imagine that
today we would say that he had had a nervous breakdown.

Then, as you began to move along the Cumberland and
Tennessee Rivers, Sherman was sent to Paducah. His job was
to forward reinforcements to you at Fort Donelson and he was
satisfied to do just that. Do you suppose that Sherman still
was reeling from his emotional problems and that he felt that
the responsibility for commanding troops in combat was
beyond his capabilities?

.... ?

Why do I say that? It's not what *I* say, it's what *he* said about
your actions at Henry and Donelson and the impact you had
on him as a soldier. He couldn't believe that the jaded
cordwood salesman he had met in St. Louis such a short time
ago could be so daring nor did he expect your brash action to
be successful. Disaster, he believed, would surely befall you.
But your win at Donelson almost miraculously relieved Sherman of his depression. I think his 1864 note to you says it all:
"Until you won at Donelson, I confess I was almost cowed by
the terrible array of anarchical elements that presented themselves at every point; but that victory admitted the ray of light
which I have followed ever since."

....

Yes, Sir, he surely was cured. By the time you arrived at
Pittsburg Landing, it appears that Sherman had shaken all
semblance of what you once called "trepidation and anxiety."
Sherman refused to see any threats to your positions at Shiloh
until the morning of April 6th. Then, too late, he was forced
to declare: "My God! We are attacked."

....

Quite right, General. Sherman may have played the ostrich in not recognizing any of the signs of an impending attack, but out of Shiloh came a bond between you and him which would change the course of American history. What do you say, shall we save Shiloh for another day?

....

That's fine with me, Sir. By the way, thanks for the cigar.

CHAPTER FOUR

*"TO WALK ON DEAD BODIES WITHOUT A FOOT
TOUCHING THE GROUND."*

Shiloh
(April 6-7, 1862)

*SYNOPSIS: After the conquest of Fort Donelson, Lincoln
made sure that Grant, his fighting general, was promoted to
major-general before any other brigadier --- then only Halleck
outranked him in the Western Theater. Grant's victory at Fort
Donelson also raised Halleck's stock and he was given command of the entire West, including Buell's department. Halleck
then planned to follow-up Grant's victory with a massive offensive against the Rebel forces in Mississippi. To this end he
ordered his various armies to unite; the meeting place (chosen
by C. F. Smith while Grant was in Halleck's doghouse) was
Pittsburg Landing, Tennessee --- also known as Shiloh Church.
Not unexpectedly, the Confederate high command could also
see Halleck's plan taking shape and had no desire to wait to be
destroyed. General Albert Sidney Johnston with his deputy,
Pierre Gustave Toutant de Beauregard, gathered up forty-
thousand men and attacked Grant's exposed Army of the Tennessee before the others arrived.*

*Shiloh turned out to be a slaughterhouse of incomparable
proportions and brought screams for Grant's head from all
quarters. The repercussions from the battle nearly drove Grant
to resign. It is conceivable that only some stern advice from
Sherman and Halleck's subsequent assignment to Washington
kept Grant on the track toward the high command.*

Here we are again, General Grant, at one of those idyllic places where the beauty of nature hides the gore that once made a tawny river run red.

... ...

Yes, Sir! This was a scene without precedent on this continent --- Antietam, Fredericksburg, Chancellorsville, and Gettysburg had not yet been fought. Losses such as those suffered at Shiloh would one day become commonplace, but what happened here on April 6th and 7th, 1862 awakened the entire country suddenly to the killing power of the Civil War armies.

... .

No, General, there was nothing like this in the war with Mexico, the War of 1812, nor the Revolution. The dead and wounded in these three conflicts amounted to some twenty-eight thousand --- and they were spread over twelve years of fighting. In the Civil War the casualties for a single battle often approached twenty-eight thousand --- and Shiloh was the first of those brutal struggles.

..... .

You're quite right, General, no one fully understood the improvements in rifles and artillery which had taken place over the previous ten years. The 1850's and 1860's marked the end of the Napoleonic battlefield and the rifled musket-barrel in particular set the stage for the modern "killingfield." My point is, the slaughter which took place at Shiloh nearly led to your being cashiered once again.

... . ?

The results of the battle may be well known, Sir; what may not be generally understood is how the outcome affected you, the other generals involved, and the prosecution of the war.

... ... ?

What do I mean? Well, let's look for a minute. The battle

and the recriminations afterward strengthened the embryonic bond between you and Sherman into a blood relationship. You demonstrated, moreover, that you could fight even when the world seemed to be crashing down around you, and that further bolstered Lincoln's faith in you. Did you know that a British general of this century wrote a book about you and made the point that after the initial surprise, your leadership at Shiloh was "... quite wonderful?"

....

I should have guessed that you'd already met General Fuller. It makes sense that he would have looked you up as soon as he could. Beyond your situation, however, the battle also built the confidence level of the green soldiers who were the bulk of the Army of the Tennessee; they saw that they could take anything the Rebels could throw at them and still win.

....

You have that right --- it also scared "Old Brains" Halleck half to death. We have to remember that "Old Brains" got both his name and most of his war experiences by reading about campaigns fought with swords, arrows or at best the "Brown Bess" smoothbore musket. With the maximum range of the smoothbore at about fifty yards (compared to at least five hundred yards for a Civil War rifled weapon), casualties such as those at Shiloh were beyond his ken. It was a safe bet that there would be no chance for a repeat occurrence once he took command of the combined armies and he was eminently successful in avoiding casualties. Of course, he also succeeded in extinguishing the spark which your victory at Donelson had kindled.

....

You often said that Corinth should have been taken in two days rather than six weeks and you stated unequivocally that prompt movements after the capture of Corinth could have resulted in "... a bloodless advance to Atlanta, to Vicksburg, or to any other desired point south of Corinth in the interior of Mississippi." What you were saying is that the war could have been shortened by at least a year and the horrendous casualties of 1864 may have been avoided. Well, Sir, it didn't happen that way. Let's look at what did happen.

As we saw, on March 4th, General C. F. Smith had been given command of your army and ordered to set up a staging area on the Tennessee River. General Buell and his Army of the Ohio were to join your troops there and, under Halleck, this combined force was expected to clear the Confederates from Mississippi. When you arrived at Pittsburg Landing you found General Smith bedridden, suffering from the infection which would soon take his life. Sherman had joined the Army of the Tennessee, commanded a division and was Smith's alter ego along the front line.

....

We're getting your message, General. This was not the timid Sherman of Ohio and Kentucky. His confidence was completely restored after he saw the Confederate bogeyman dissolve at Donelson; now Sherman could not see a sign of the enemy anywhere and with no enemy in sight, neither he nor General Smith saw any need for entrenchments.

....

So Smith's words to you were, "By God, I want nothing better than to have the Rebels come out and attack us! We can whip them to hell. Our men suppose we have come here to fight, and if we begin to spade, it will make them think we fear the enemy." Now we can see what happened. You listened to Sherman, and you both listened to Smith --- after all, the old commandant was a man before whom you and Sherman stood in awe.

As the day of reckoning drew closer, however, Sherman would prove to be your real problem. He had told you that General Johnston had twenty thousand troops at Corinth, Mississippi --- in fact he had forty thousand. When a journalist asked Sherman why he appeared to be so blase about the possibility of danger, he replied, "Oh, they'd only call me crazy again." On other occasions he'd pass off the danger with, "Beauregard is not such a fool as to leave his base of operation and attack us in ours." One thing was certain, he was going to show his fellow officers that he was well cured of his "cowardly lion" syndrome.

... .

I'll say you agreed with him, General Grant. Long after the battle you wrote, "The fact is, I regarded the campaign we were engaged in as an offensive one and had no idea that the enemy would leave strong intrenchments to take the initiative when he knew he would be attacked where he was if he remained." But, General, doesn't this contradict the very logic you used to justify your rapid movement on Fort Donelson? Then you said, "...15,000 men on the 8th would be more effective than 50,000 a month later."

... ...

No, General, that situation wasn't that much different. Albert Sidney Johnston was a proud and competent general who was virtually in disgrace for losing almost all of Kentucky and Tennessee in just a month. As he looked from his Corinth trenches, he could see massive reinforcements marching toward Pittsburg Landing. As you had decided to hit Donelson before it could be reinforced, so Johnston hoped to smash the Army of the Tennessee before the Army of the Ohio arrived. Would you have waited to be attacked by an enemy whose strength was building?

....

I didn't think so. What it really comes down to is that persistent feeling you had that only U. S. Grant could take the offensive. When the Rebels attacked at Donelson you said, "... I had no idea that there would be any engagement on land unless I brought it on myself." When it came to playing the ostrich at Shiloh, both you and Sherman can claim an Academy Award.

....?

You're absolutely right, General, I *am* talking about the prize for the year's best actor and actress. You certainly do keep up with things wherever you are now --- but shall we get back to Shiloh?

... .

Good! On the evening of April 5th, Sherman had advised you that he was experiencing a good deal of shooting along the picket line; however, he made it clear: "I do not apprehend anything like an attack on our position." The next morning the roof fell in and Sherman uttered his prize understatement: "My God! We are attacked."

..... .

So, you heard the thunder of the guns nine miles away where you were waiting for General Buell to arrive. You seemed to sense that it was a big affair. "Gentleman," you said matter of factly, "the ball is in motion. Let's be off." With only a brief stop at Crump's Landing enroute to advise General Lew Wallace to start his division moving toward the sound of the guns, at eight in the morning you stepped into the bloodbath at Shiloh Church.

....?

Eyewitness descriptions of the scene at Pittsburg Landing are so bizarre that I really can't imagine how the scene appeared to you as you rode down the gangplank. Fully, one third of your command was out of the battle as hordes of the raw recruits had fled to the protective cover of the river bank.

... ...

Are you serious, General? You mean to say that when you asked a young soldier why he was running away he answered, "Because I can't fly." That was quite an introduction to the battle --- at least it gave you some idea of the panic which had overwhelmed your young soldiers.

... .

That's worth noting, General --- if one third took off from the fighting, then the remaining two thirds put up a glorious fight. They had fallen back about a mile, but they had kept the semblance of order. The Rebels had not been able to make a breakthrough nor roll up a flank. I can see why you think that for raw soldiers they weren't too shabby.

... ...

I see your point. Johnston's troops were no more ex-perienced or disciplined than the Army of the Tennessee. That was probably what saved the day for you. All through the day the Union line bent back toward the river; however, it would not break. Pockets of resistance all along the line stopped the Confederate's momentum as the onrushing troops paused to mop them up. One of these spots went into history as the "Hornet's Nest."

... .

Yes, Sir, that's the place which you told General Prentiss to hold at all hazards and his division held out for most of the day. Night came and the fighting stopped, and the skies poured down a flat-rock rain. Buell's army had arrived and you recalled from what you had seen in Mexico and Donelson that, when both sides seemed fought out, the army that could pull itself together for one last push would win the day.

... .

So you knew all the time that you would whip them in the morning. Buell didn't think so. He thought that a retreat was in order. General McPherson was not sanguine about continuing the fight --- and he was not a member of the faint-of-heart club of generals. Perhaps Sherman and you were the only two who realized that opportunity, not disaster, was knocking.

....

Maybe not even Sherman? It really surprises me to hear you say that. It wasn't until years later that he admitted that he had a reservation. Frankly, General, when he finally did own up, you were not in a position to hear him --- it was eight years after you had ... ummm ...

....?

No, I'm not afraid to say it ... after you had died. Anyway, he met you that evening and before he could even bring up the subject of fight or retreat, you immediately restored his confidence with a muttered, "Lick 'em tomorrow." This may have been the first manifestation of what Lincoln would later call "... that dogged persistence of Grant's."

At the end of the first day, both sides were assessing the situation. Albert Sidney Johnston was dead. General Beauregard had succeeded to command (the same Beauregard who had fired the war's first shot at Fort Sumter just an eternal year before this cataclysmic battle) and he saw an army that was fought out, disorganized, and bewildered --- the troops unable to fathom why, despite their apparent successes of the 6th, they were never quite able to overwhelm the battered Yankees. Beauregard's observations convinced him that the time had come to save his army for another day while it was still a cohesive force.

....

Yes, General, you attacked on the morning of the 7th; the

Confederates still fought stubbornly, but time had run out for them. By mid-afternoon they were dragging themselves back to Corinth. A short time later you toured the battlefield and observed: "I saw an open field in our possession on the second day, over which the Confederates had made repeated charges the day before, so covered with dead that it would have been possible to walk across the clearing, in any direction, stepping on dead bodies, without a foot touching the ground." It's no wonder that you seldom hear the battle called just "Shiloh." It's always "Bloody Shiloh."

.. ..

No, Sir, I won't forget the question of pursuit. That was only one of the criticisms heaped upon you in the aftermath of this battle. However, this one may have some validity. You tried to get Sherman and McClernand to rally their troops and make a vigorous pursuit, but the Army of the Tennessee was too played out. Then you "invited" Buell to....

....

I understand, General, the command line between you and Buell was tenuous at best. Soon Halleck would be arriving to control both armies, so you didn't think it appropriate that you *order* Buell's fresh troops to harass the retreating enemy. One thing for certain, General Grant, without an order there was nothing under God's blue sky which would have persuaded Don Carlos Buell, a charter member of the Napoleon Club, to put his troops in harm's way.

You know, the best conclusion I have heard about that frightful day was Sherman's: "I assure you, my dear fellow, that we had quite enough of their society for two whole days, and were only too glad to be rid of them on any terms."

... .

General, you may think that Sherman's quip says it all, but I don't. There's still quite a bit to say about this battle. At first it was proclaimed a glorious victory for the Union and "Unconditional Surrender" Grant. Then the unbelievable casualty lists started surfacing and certain "sinister forces" among the military began to pass highly uncomplimentary remarks to the press about the way you handled the battle. Many of these comments have been attributed to Buell and those close to him. I suppose that you've read Buell's article in *Century Magazine* or *Battles and Leaders*? It tells a different story than your commentary. The charges raised by your hidden detractors included unwarranted surprise, alcohol abuse, away from your post, and sheer incompetence.

....

Of course what they were saying were products of an evil imagination. The times given for your arrival at the battlefield and Prentiss's surrender at the "Hornet's Nest," for instance, were wildly in error. The reasons bandied about for Lew Wallace's late arrival were equally spurious. The end result was a flow of letters to Washington alternately condemning or praising your actions on that fateful day. In the end it came down to President Lincoln listening to an impassioned plea for your removal, but, after pausing in deep thought, he whispered earnestly to your detractor, "I can't spare this man. He fights.!"

....?

Yes, General, I know whom Lincoln said that to. It was A. K. McClure, a prominent Pennsylvania Republican. He was partly responsible for swinging the Pennsylvania delegation to Lincoln at the 1860 convention. The fact of the matter was that he was passing on a request from Leonard Swett that Lincoln sack you.

....?

Leonard Swett? Yes I've heard of him too. He was a close friend of Lincoln's and one of the campaign managers who was instrumental in securing the Republican nomination for him. You know, General, I have the feeling that you have something more than the convention in mind.

... .

Of course! Swett was one of those conniving contractors you threatened to shoot if he didn't leave your Illinois military district. He complained to Lincoln about you, but Lincoln backed you all the way --- even advising Swett to stay clear of you; you were the type of man who might just carry out that threat to have him shot.

So you believe that a large part of this conspiracy against you was motivated by disillusioned money-grabbers of which Swett and McClure were examples. What was it that people said of the war? A rich man's war but a poor man's fight? I suppose that's the way it has always been --- and always will be.

... .

Yes, Sir, "... and always will be." Now let's look at the impact of the battle. I think you'll agree that had the army been dug in and had Sherman been just a little less convinced that there was no chance of an attack, you may have dealt Johnston's army a disastrous defeat. Then the entire Mississippi Valley would have been ripe for the picking.

... ...

Yes, it's certainly true that the defeat which you did inflict on Beauregard was enough to open the door to the Valley, but Shiloh scared the "good old boys" into the only safe posture they knew --- inaction. Isn't it strange that the great triumvirate, "Little Mac," "Old Brains,"and the suave Don Carlos, all cast in the image of Napoleon, among them would not win a decisive offensive victory at any time during the war.

... .

I'm sure that you have heard enough about these losers. The

more important fact which comes through loud and clear is your changing opinion of the nature of the war. After Donelson and the massive Confederate retreat, you thought that the enemy was thoroughly demoralized. This all changed when you saw them mount such a fierce offensive --- that was not a demoralized group which tore through your camps at Shiloh. ....

What was it that you said later?

Up to the battle of Shiloh I ... believed that the rebellion against the government would collapse suddenly and soon, if a decisive victory could be gained over any of its armies. Donelson and Henry were such victories. An army of 20,000 men was captured or destroyed. Bowling Green, Columbus, Hickman, Clarksville, and Nashville also fell into our hands. The Tennessee and Cumberland Rivers, from their mouths to the head of navigation, were secured. But when Confederate armies were collected ... assumed the offensive and made such a gallant effort to regain what had been lost, then indeed, I gave up all idea of saving the Union except by complete conquest.

That was not all. Do you remember how you translated this doctrine of conquest into what we now call total war? Listen to your own words again:

Up to that time, it had been the policy of the army, certainly that portion commanded by me, to protect the property of citizens whose territory was invaded, without regard to their sentiments, whether Union or Secession. After this, however, I regarded it as humane to both sides to protect the persons of those found in their homes, but to consume everything that could be used to support or supply armies ... such supplies within the reach of the Confederate Armies I regarded as much as contraband as arms or ordnance stores. ... This policy, I believe, exercised a material influence in hastening the end.

This little excerpt tells a momentous story. It was a decisive change in the way war was waged. No longer would the rules of Frederick the Great --- mercenary armies against mercenary armies --- apply. From that time on the enemy's total capacity for supporting a war became legitimate military targets. The theory, purely twentieth century, became known as "total war."

... .

I wouldn't have expected you to think about it in that way back in the 1800's. But you and Sherman started a revolutionary system of warfare which, particularly with the advent of nuclear weapons, finally may have made war between the major powers too costly to pursue.

We mentioned before that Shiloh took its toll on your relations with Halleck. More than ever, he was convinced that you were no soldier, but he wasn't about to tangle with President Lincoln again. His answer was what we call "kicking the man upstairs" --- give someone a title that sounds and looks important but be sure to restrict his responsibilities to only trivial matters. He made you his deputy with no direct command responsibility unless the commanding general himself was killed.

... .

I suppose that you're right --- there was no chance of Halleck getting killed since there would be no fight. That meant that if you were ever again going to have command of troops in the field he would have to die of old age. This situation was a bitter pill for you to swallow and you were on the verge of a drastic action. Sherman claims that you were about to resign from the army when he persuaded you otherwise. You merely note that you had repeatedly asked to be relieved from duty under Halleck and that that was the substance of your discussion with Sherman. Old friends on your staff thought that an independent command along the Atlantic Coast would have been an appropriate assignment and ...

... .

I didn't think that you were aware that several of them had written to Congressman Washburne to request his assistance. That wasn't your way at all. Your old superstition about not finagling an assignment would have prevented you from seeking the Congressman's help. What was it you said: "... in positions of great responsibility every one should do his duty to the best of his ability where assigned by competent authority, without application or the use of influence to change his position."

As it turned out, the whole matter became academic as one of those peculiar "fortuitous circumstances" we discussed earlier suddenly came into play: Halleck himself was kicked upstairs. Lincoln named him to replace McClellan as the Commanding General of the Armies. You then became the Commander of the Department of Mississippi.

... ...

I understand that the job was more title than substance. The Department had been emasculated from what it had been when Halleck was in command. As you said: "The magnificent army of 120,000 which entered Corinth on the 30th of May had now become so scattered that I was put entirely on the defensive in a territory whose population was hostile to the Union."

... .

So, with your troops spread all over the Southwest doing guard duty, you were unable to mount an offensive. Earl Van Dorn was building up a force that you estimated at thirty-five to forty thousand. He could have hit you at any place and you would have been hard pressed to defend against him. This, you claimed, was your most anxious period of the war.

..... .

True, the momentum which the Federals generated with the move on Donelson in February was quickly ebbing. Buell had been ordered to move his Army of the Ohio back to Chattanooga. He moved, however, with the speed of a Halleck and never posed a threat to General Bragg's Confederates. Bragg simply ignored Buell and arrogantly marched through Kentucky to the Ohio River.

What had looked so secure for the Union gave every indication of falling apart and Washington was again in a panic. As you watched the work of the previous year go down the drain, you felt that your Army of the Tennessee would have been more advantageously employed had Halleck allowed you to move to the offensive rather than remaining on the defensive to "... hold a force far inferior to my own."

..... .

So, you're telling me that finally a breakthrough came. The old politician, Major-General John McClernand, sold Lincoln on a brainstorm of his --- he would go to Illinois, raise an army and use it to capture Vicksburg. If Halleck despised anyone more than yourself, it was one of the political generals on a glory trip. He was not in a position to reveal all that was being planned in Washington, but in response to your query of November 10th, 1862, Halleck finally unlocked your shackles: "You have command of all troops sent to your department [including those recruited by McClernand] and have permission to fight the enemy where you please."

..... .

You're probably right, General. "Pontius Pilate" Halleck was washing his hands of the entire scheme and making the care and feeding of McClernand your problem. There was no way "Old Brains" would get himself between the President, Lincoln's favorite fighting-general and this very necessary

Illinois politician. But no matter what prompted it, General, you were free to move the Army of the Tennessee on to Vicksburg --- even if you had to race McClernand's private army to the town.

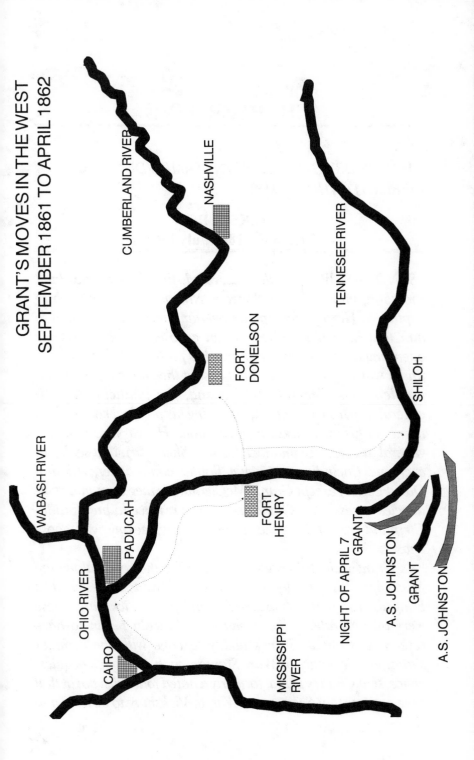

GRANT'S MOVES IN THE WEST
SEPTEMBER 1861 TO APRIL 1862

WABASH RIVER

OHIO RIVER

CAIRO

PADUCAH

MISSISSIPPI RIVER

CUMBERLAND RIVER

NASHVILLE

FORT DONELSON

FORT HENRY

TENNESEE RIVER

SHILOH

NIGHT OF APRIL 7
GRANT

A.S. JOHNSTON

GRANT

A.S. JOHNSTON

CHAPTER FIVE

"I WAS ON DRY GROUND ON THE SAME SIDE OF THE RIVER WITH THE ENEMY."

VICKSBURG
(December 1862-July 1863)

SYNOPSIS: While Halleck dawdled, the Confederates built Vicksburg into a massive fortress. Now it was Grant's job to capture it. His first attempt, an overland movement, proved to him that he could not rely on an exposed supply line while operating deep in enemy territory. His problem then became to find a way to get to the dry land east of the citadel. His second problem was General McClernand, the politician-turned-general who, as we've noted, was using his political connections to mount his own Vicksburg expedition. He was now a major-general, a corps commander (as was Sherman), and senior to everyone (including the naval flotilla commander, Admiral David Porter) except Grant. McClernand's megalomaniac tendencies necessitated Grant's constant presence to prevent McClernand from taking the army on glory seeking wild goose chases.

As Grant waited through the winter for the roads along the Mississippi River to dry, he tried several bypasses designed to bring his army to that treasured dry land east of Vicksburg. These were all miserable failures and even Lincoln began to have reservations about Grant's ability to cope with the complex situation. Secretary of War Stanton, with Lincoln's acquiescence, sent Charles Dana, formerly a noted journalist but at that time an Assistant Secretary of War, to Vicksburg to observe and report on Grant's conduct. Dana became a Grant supporter to the end of the war.

Grant's daring Vicksburg maneuver, taking a large army deep into enemy territory without a secure line back to a supply area, would never have been approved by Halleck in Washington had he known what was about to take place. Grant, therefore, used his favorite device --- tell the boss what he is about to do and challenge the chief to tell him to stop. Of course he fully expected that the situation would be resolved before the messages could complete the round trip. When Grant finally heard from Halleck, some three weeks later, he was about to begin the Vicksburg siege.

Good morning, General Grant, we've certainly covered a lot of territory so far. We began at Belmont and now we're on the bluffs of Vicksburg. In 1863 this area was described as Jefferson Davis's "Gibraltar of the West."

... .

That's very true --- right after Shiloh, Vicksburg was a ripe plum waiting to be picked. But "Old Brains" Halleck squandered that opportunity and gave the Confederates time to build a massive fort on the heights overlooking that big bend in the Mississippi. As long as the Confederate artillery dominated these heights, Mark Twain's river was useless as a waterway. As the last days of 1862 dwindled into the winter of 1863, it became obvious that only an all-out campaign would wrest the fortress from Confederate control --- that is if a workable plan could even be devised.

... ...

That's a good idea. General. If we describe the terrain around Vicksburg, then everyone can understand why it was so difficult to capture.

First, there is the Mississippi River itself. The great river doesn't really flow from Minnesota to the Gulf of Mexico; rather it coils and uncoils like a giant python as it twists its way through the midsection of the continent. And, like a slithering serpent, the coils can change direction in only the seconds it takes for a raging thunderstorm to dump its watery cargo somewhere upstream or just as certainly, if more slowly, as the spring thaw melts the snows a thousand miles to the north.

Even in the days of the nineteenth century, man had tried to control this monster of a river with dikes and levees; however, in the end the river always won. A sudden rainstorm and the water would explode through the dams to reclaim the swamps and estuaries of which it had been master. When change did come, it was the river which ultimately forced the evolution with Darwinian persistence. Man could harness, man could use, but man has never been able to control this silt-filled beast indefinitely. When man tried to show *his* power, the river would eventually counter with an irresistible fury and a new river would be born.

In the 1860's, as we can see on the map, the river came gliding towards Vicksburg from the northwest, then made a right angle turn to the northeast. After three miles of flowing on this course, the river reversed itself 180 degrees and, resuming its inexorable journey to the sea, streamed to the southwest. At the apex of the curve formed by the river's reversal, a significant tributary, the Yazoo, emptied into the main river. At this point the high ground began, and the Rebels had fortified every yard of the promontory along the Mississippi for the next ten miles.

... .

No, Sir, I won't forget to tell them about the area around Vicksburg. The muck and swamps which circled the northern sector were the source of all of your problems. To say the

Yazoo emptied into the Mississippi does not really do justice to the tributary's terminus --- a tangled forest of stagnant water and grotesque swamp trees which rivaled Okefenokee or the Everglades. In reality, the Yazoo oozed, not flowed, into the Mississippi.

As the Yazoo wandered down from the northeast to the Mississippi, its northerly bank was a saturation of aimless creeks, bayous, and marshlands. Across the stream, however, extending from Vicksburg for some thirty miles, a steep ridge rose above the low lying swampland. From these heights, Confederate artillery could dominate any invader approaching from the north.

The city of Vicksburg itself was laid out an a precipice two hundred feet above the Mississippi River. A threatening army could march unmenaced to a point on the western shore of the Mississippi opposite the citadel. There it would be less than a mile from the city, nevertheless, it might as well have been on the moon. No force under the sun could have crossed under the barrels of the Confederate guns, no artillery of that day could have threatened the enemy's batteries and no ships, it was thought, could have withstood the brutal battering expected from the Confederate guns should they attempt to navigate the river in front of Vicksburg.

... .

All right, General, I'll get to Port Hudson. Port Hudson was the other remaining Confederate stronghold on the river. Situated some one hundred and twenty miles south of Vicksburg, it effectively prevented the Union Navy from approaching Vicksburg from Baton Rouge. So, General, you had steamships above Vicksburg and below Port Hudson and neither fleet appeared able to assist you in getting your army to the dry land south of Vicksburg. Does that about sum up the situation as you saw it in December of 1862?

....

Good! You felt then that the only way to Vicksburg was from the east --- a direct attack meant marching 150 miles from Memphis through enemy territory with the very real probability that a raider like Bedford Forrest would smash your supply lines. You also had to face the problem of an enemy within your lines as well as without --- you could never forget the lurking shadow of the political general, John Mc-Clernand.

McClernand, an Illinois Democrat and former Congressman, saw the war as an opportunity --- an opportunity for glory which would later translate into votes, perhaps even presidential votes. Lincoln, needing support from all quarters, was anxious to appease McClernand and the other politicians who swelled the Union Army's senior ranks. In late 1862, with General Halleck using his armies to occupy territory rather than to win a war, General McClernand saw his chance for glory --- lead a Federal army into Vicksburg.

As you said, General McClernand persuaded Lincoln that he had a plan and the President gave him the authority to proceed.

....

That's very important, Sir. Thanks for the reminder. Lincoln, Stanton and Halleck had not gone completely balmy over McClernand. At least he was not going to operate in your department as an independent army, he would be subordinate and responsible to you. As the campaign proceeded, this provision by Washington proved to be the glue which kept the whole operation together.

....

Right, General, we are getting ahead of ourselves again. Your first inclination then, was to capture Vicksburg outright before McClernand came onto the scene. As you say, politics makes strange bedfellows. Your tormentor, Halleck, had a great aversion to the political generals with whom he was forced to deal. Even *you* were preferable to one of them, so you had an advisor sneaking crumbs of information to you which, in turn, helped you to keep one step ahead of Mc-Clernand. But it also drove you to try the overland invasion which proved to be a fiasco.

....

I'm not disputing that it was a good plan, General. It's just that in order for it to work, everything had to go exactly as planned --- you made no allowance for Murphy's law.

... .

No General, not that Murphy. The fact that a Colonel Murphy undermined your entire campaign is just a coincidence. Let me explain. Murphy's law is wry humor. It states that in any planned activity if something can possibly go wrong, it will. Now, it just happened that the colonel who commanded at your Holly Springs depot (where something most assuredly went wrong) was R. C. Murphy of the 8th Wisconsin and we'll get to him in a minute. First I want to hear about your plan of operations.

....

So, you hoped to stymie any direct enemy movements against you by making a two-pronged drive toward Vicksburg: Your army invading from the North, Sherman's force from the river. You expected that the enemy would move north to meet you. Then, with all the Confederate attention focused on your activity, Sherman's corps would steam down the Mississippi, into the Yazoo River, across Chickasaw Bluffs and sweep into a virtually undefended city.

....

I wasn't trying to imply that it was as simple as that. After all, it was a cooperative movement --- and a most difficult cooperative movement because once the ball was in motion it would become almost impossible for you and Sherman to communicate. As you reported the plan: "I hoped to hold Pemberton in my front while Sherman should get in his rear and into Vicksburg. The further north the enemy could be held the better ... if Pemberton could not be held away from Vicksburg I was to follow him." As I said, it basically was a good but chancy plan, then Murphy's law --- and Murphy himself --- stopped you dead in your tracks.

... .!

Wow! you still have it in for Colonel Murphy. Of course you have good reason. As you said, once before he had let you down, and, after he had begged forgiveness, you gave him another chance. Unfortunately, he happened to be the officer who wound up in command of your main supply depot in Mississippi when your old nemesis, Earl Van Dorn, arrived with 3,500 raiders. No one can describe your feelings better than yourself: "*On the 20th [of December 1862] General Van Dorn appeared at Holly Springs, captured the garrison of 1,500 commanded by Colonel Murphy of the 8th Wisconsin, and destroyed all our ammunition and forage. The capture was a disgraceful one to the officer commanding. [The] surrender of Holly Springs was most reprehensible and showed either the disloyalty of Colonel Murphy to the cause which he professed to serve. or gross cowardice.*" I never knew that you could be so subtle, General....

.. ..

Careful now, remember your rule about swearing, but I must admit that Murphy did leave you and your army between the proverbial rock and a hard place. Even more, Sherman was out of touch with the Union forces. He didn't know that you had been forced to abandon your advance and had to fall back to where your troops could be resupplied. The hapless Sherman arrived at Chickasaw Bluffs expecting to have the place to himself or, at the very least, to find your contingent pressing the enemy from the east. In a word, Sherman's men were hammered. He took eighteen hundred casualties because of the cowardice of a single man. As you said when you discussed Sherman's unaided attack: "The Rebel position was impregnable against any force that could be brought against its front."

... .

It really was an opportunity lost. Winter was setting in and a campaign in the rainy season in Mississippi was virtually out of the question. The Union leadership situation had changed, too. McClernand, who at that time outranked all of the Union generals but yourself, had arrived on the scene and it wasn't long before Sherman and Admiral Porter were screaming for you to assume command at the front. McClernand, they declared together, was insufferable.

... .

That's an excellent point, General. It's worth stopping for a moment to go back for another look at the Colonel Murphy situation --- in the long run, he and Van Dorn may have done you a big favor at Holly Springs. The attack had wiped out your Army's rations and forage; however, you solved the problem simply enough --- the fields of Mississippi were a cornucopia of food and the soldiers simply collected their rations from the abundance of the local farms. You even said that you learned a lesson which you took advantage of later in the campaign and you finally came to believe that the supplies lost at Holly Springs were "... more than compensated for by ... the lesson taught."

... .

Yes, Sir, I see what you mean --- in January of 1863 the seed of an idea was planted in your mind and it grew into the plan which you used to take Vicksburg four months later. Months after Vicksburg had fallen, this same seed nourished Sherman's thinking as he departed Atlanta in 1864. But for the present, the idea which was growing would eventually take you on one of the most audacious military maneuvers in American history. While waiting for the fruit to ripen, however, you had to keep in motion. As a result, you tried four separate maneuvers to get around Vicksburg's bluffs--- each of which was a dismal failure.

....

You certainly did pay a price for the failures. The newspapers had found the perfect whipping boy for all that had gone wrong anywhere in the country over the past few months --- *YOU* ! It must have seemed that you were hearing old Jesse Grant's fatherly jibes all over again.

... .

No, there's no reason to talk about Jesse Grant now. Let's stay with the campaign. I'll just say that it must have been painful to you because twenty years later you detailed the tales in your *MEMOIRS*. You admitted to being excoriated as idle, incompetent and unfit to command men and, beyond name calling, many of your enemies cried out for you to be replaced.

... .

Oh, you say it was worse than just being replaced --- each newspaper seemed to have its own champion to tout. Names bandied about included two who already had been found wanting in far less demanding situations --- Frémont and Hunter; McClellan's name surfaced, of course, and also that of the most ambitious of all of the politicians-turned-general, the commander of your XIII Corps, John McClernand.

... ...

Political generals certainly were the bane of your existence for the entire war. McClernand was a serious problem at at that moment. Then, once you finally got across the river,

Nathaniel Banks would be the problem as he failed to meet the schedule established for a cooperative movement. Later in the war, General Ben Butler, a critical Massachusetts politician, would fail miserably in what may have been a glorious opportunity end the war in mid-1864.

....

Of course you would have preferred to get rid of them, but you certainly understood that these political flights of fancy had to be endured as long as their encouragement helped to sustain the people's will to continue the war. If appeasing these arrogant glory seekers meant the unnecessary killing of a few rank and file soldiers, this unfortunate exchange had to be acceptable to Lincoln.

... .

All right --- back to Vicksburg. From the aftermath of Shiloh until you were south of the citadel you endured the taunts patiently. You may have ended them by disclosing your plans and satisfying the fourth estate. Let's be honest though, had they heard what you really intended to do come April, they may have declared you as insane as they had once said Sherman was. Surprisingly, you accepted their scourgings meekly: "Your newspaper is very unjust to me; but time will make it all right," you said, "I only want to be judged by my acts." Very modest, very mild, but just a hint that the bitter remarks did hurt.

... .

I didn't know that you were a Shakespeare scholar, General. Is that what you were doing at West Point when you should have been studying tactics, reading Shakespeare? But you're so right. It *was* the winter of your discontent --- and a miserable time for your troops. The lowlands were flooded; the men were forced to sleep wet, work wet and eat wet; victims of dystentary, small pox, malaria, and even measles swelled the sick lists. As the accusations piled up, your most conscientious supporter, President Lincoln, began to have some doubts about his fighting general on the river.

To ease his concerns, Lincoln conspired with the crusty Secretary of War Stanton to do a little spying in Mississippi. Remember? In our first conversation we talked about them sending Charles A. Dana to your headquarters to report on what was really happening. As it turned out, he was the best thing that had happened to you since you teamed with Sherman. His first report condemned the scheming McClernand as a less than first rate field officer, but, more importantly, Washington's reply, in effect, made McClernand expendable for the cause. We also know now that Dana also convinced Washington that the rumors about your drinking habits were just that --- rumors.

....

Yes, General, I do keep bringing up the drinking thing and you are still trying to sweep it under the rug. Whether you like it or not, it was a real problem for you. If the powers in Washington had believed the wild stories being spread around, you would have been the ex-commander of the Army of the Tennessee. Look at a simple case. You remember General Thayer, don't you? He commanded a brigade in your army. It happened that he was visiting Washington and had a session with Lincoln at the White House. Lincoln's first question, as Thayer reported it, was "Does Grant ever get drunk?" Thayer, fortunately, pleaded your case and called you a much maligned man. "What I want is generals who will fight battles and win victories. Grant has done that and I propose to stand by him," Lincoln told Thayer. You can see that it took people such as Dana and Thayer to convince the President that you deserved his trust?

I think that it's time to look at your plan-of-the-month club and I suspect we will find that even people of good will had reason to wonder what was happening on the river. You already had one failure as a result of the Holly Springs surrender, then you tried the canal across the peninsula in front of Vicksburg.

....

So what if the canal was Lincoln's idea. You certainly couldn't tell anybody outside of your immediate circle that the President considered himself another Mark Twain when it came to understanding the Mississippi. It's true enough that had the river behaved like a normal river and followed the engineers' rules of hydrodynamics you would have been able to send the steamships south of Vicksburg without running the gauntlet of Rebel guns. But we have to be honest, General, anyone not in the know could hardly be faulted, as he watched thousands of men standing in waist deep mud trying to dredge a waterway, for believing that a lunatic was running the show.

After the canal failed, you tried to find a route west of the city by way of Lake Providence, Louisiana. McPherson, formerly the army's engineer and now a corps commander, worked his corps for a month on the project before he advised you to give it up.

....

As you say, all of this was a way for keeping the men busy and those troops who went to Lake Providence were happy to get away from the swamps for a while. However, to the carping observers each case simply looked like another Grant inspired disaster.

We can't forget the two military moves through the bayous and swamps north of bluffs --- your excursions through such unlikely avenues as the Tallahatchie River, Steele's Bayou and the Yazoo River not only proved the folly of trying to wage

war in these backwaters, but on two occasions very nearly cost
Admiral Porter his fleet.

..... .

General, I didn't say that these were altogether bad ideas ---
had one of them worked it would have been hailed as an
ingenious plan. I'm talking about perceptions --- can you deny
that several of these fiascoes looked more like the Keystone
Kops...

..... ?

Sorry, General, I should have realized that you would not be
familiar with the Kops --- let me put it this way: More like a
minstrel show than a military operation.

....

You're right, General, as Spring approached things were
starting to break right. Dana and your colleagues Sherman
and Admiral Porter understood the problems and supported
you, the men had not lost confidence, and slowly the
newspapers even took on a more mellow tone. With Spring
would come the dry roads, and as Lincoln so proudly said of
you, you would then fight. From that seed planted after Holly
Springs, the plan began to grow and take shape. One problem
still seemed insurmountable --- getting the Navy's ships south
of Vicksburg to ferry the troops and supplies from the west to
the east bank. The Navy appeared to be out of the picture as
long as the rebels controlled the guns at Port Hudson and
Vicksburg.

.. ..

Oh, I'll say that you were lucky to have a fire-eater like
Admiral Porter to work with --- he was the reincarnation of
the indefatigable Admiral Foote of Henry and Donelson.
Porter was the first person you approached with your plan ---
without his support you could forget the whole idea. "Did he
believe that, using cotton bales, logs or anything else he could

think of as armor against the Rebel cannon balls, his ships could make a night run under the Vicksburg guns?" you asked. Porter, that fighting optimist, assured you that he would find a way. Then you turned to your second problem --- how to feed and supply the troops when they were maneuvering to the east of Vicksburg.

....

Yes, that problem was easy, thanks to Van Dorn. You knew that your army had subsisted in Mississippi once without a problem, there was no reason why the farms of Mississippi couldn't join the Union cause again. The army would carry the ammunition it needed, the good people of Mississippi would provide the rest.

....

So, only Porter, Rawlins and, of all people, McClernand thought that your plan had a prayer of success. The plan *was* daring --- certainly not one for the faint of heart. Even Sherman, who was to become one of the most unorthodox of military commanders, tried to dissuade you: "Stop all troops till your army is partially supplied with wagons ... this road will be jammed as sure as your life if you attempt to supply 50,000 men by one single road." Here you were, cut off from any base of supplies or assistance, maneuvering between two enemy armies, and your most trusted lieutenant didn't really understand your intentions.

....

So you say that Sherman may have been worried, but in fact you were relieved by your situation. I see it now. Despite the fact that you were deep in enemy territory, with a vast river and the stronghold of Vicksburg between your army and any Union assistance, the ultimate purpose of all that maneuvering since December had been realized. As you said: "I was on dry ground on the same side of the river with the enemy." So,

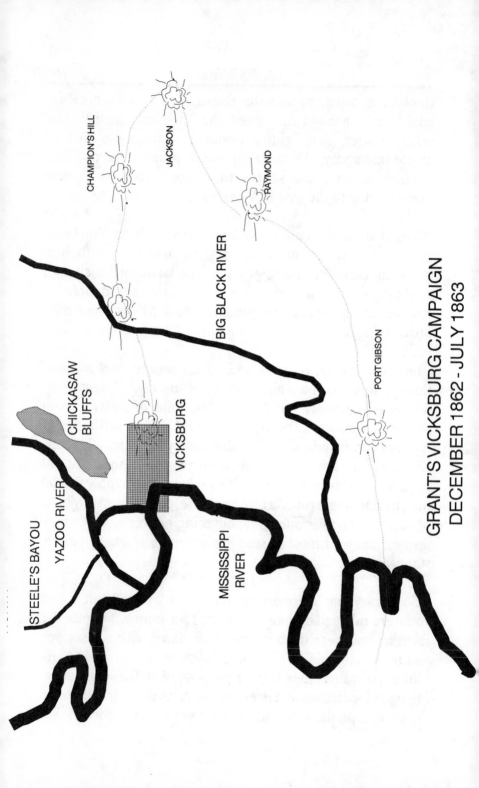

STEELE'S BAYOU

YAZOO RIVER

CHICKASAW BLUFFS

VICKSBURG

MISSISSIPPI RIVER

CHAMPION'S HILL

JACKSON

RAYMOND

BIG BLACK RIVER

PORT GIBSON

GRANT'S VICKSBURG CAMPAIGN
DECEMBER 1862 - JULY 1863

you were where you wanted to be --- let's see what you did then.

Simply stated, after you had the army across the river, you drove the men on a two hundred mile campaign, fought five battles against two different enemy armies, picked up six thousand prisoners, ninety cannon, captured the Mississippi state capital, and eighteen days later had thirty thousand Confederate soldiers penned inside of Vicksburg. In retrospect, the results appear to have been remarkable --- and so they were. However, what was really remarkable was the way it was accomplished.

Your plan had everything: Audacity, deception, execution, and above all, speed. Deception came on two fronts, Sherman's early feint at Chickasaw Bluffs which fooled poor, conventional Pemberton completely. Your old friend, with whom you had so successfully shelled the Mexican army at Chapultepec, couldn't bring himself to believe that you would operate between two enemy armies without a supply line. In Pemberton's mind, Sherman's move had to be the main attack. The second deceptive move came deep within Mississippi and baffled the entire Confederate high command. That was Grierson's six hundred mile long calvary raid. It stirred up precisely the alarms which you had intended. The final result was that Pemberton felt obligated to stay riveted to the Vicksburg fortifications --- and you had that minuscule head start which you needed to push Joe Johnston's small army out of the state capital at Jackson.

....

That's true enough, Sir. You couldn't operate against Vicksburg with Johnston's divisions in your rear. The first priority had to be to clear that area before turning toward the stronghold on the river.

On the road you must have been something to see. This was no plodding, bludgeon of a soldier --- everything was speed, speed, speed. It was in your orders: "Do this with all expedition, in 48 hours from receipt of these orders. ..." "Everything depends on the promptitude with which our supplies are forwarded." To Sherman: "See that the men's rations last five days. It is unnecessary to remind you of the overwhelming importance of celerity in your movements." On the march, the soldiers seemed to see you everywhere: "Move along men, push right along --- we must fight the enemy before our rations fail."

....

So, you still remember that when the hapless Pemberton did come poking out from his trenches, your audacity had him completely confounded. He reconnoitered toward the Mississippi River looking for your lines of communication. He couldn't find what didn't exist, could he? With the realization that he had been fooled, Pemberton rolled north to intercept your line of march. Twice he placed his forces in your path and twice the Army of the Tennessee sent the defenders reeling. In a bound, you were across the Big Black River and Pemberton had pulled back into the Vicksburg entrenchments to await the inevitable.

....

Yes, I had forgotten about Halleck completely. After all he was the Chief of the Armies and you should have had his approval for your venture. Poor old Halleck thought that you were going to cross the river and join forces with General Banks for a move against Port Hudson. I don't think that you ever had any idea of teaming up with an albatross like Banks, but the instructions from higher up stated that the marches against Port Hudson and Vicksburg were to have been cooperative assaults. Remember? You had tentatively agreed to McClernand joining in Banks's attack on Port Hudson while the remainder of your army waited for them to join you. Banks, as was true with most Union generals, couldn't keep to the timetable --- he reported that he would be delayed a month. You now had your excuse. Why don't you tell the rest, General: "I therefore determined to move independently of Banks, cut loose from my base, destroy the rebel force in the rear of Vicksburg and invest or capture the city ... the authorities in Washington were notified."

Sure they were! It was Fort Donelson all over again, wasn't it? Halleck was notified --- that was tantamount to approval as far as you were concerned. Why? "I knew well that Halleck's caution would lead him to disapprove of this course; but it was the only one that gave any chance of success. The time it would take to communicate with Washington and get a reply would be so great that I could not be interfered with until it was demonstrated whether my plan was practicable." A reprise of the "15,000 today would be better that 50,000 in a month" logic at Donelson where: "A delay would give the enemy time to reinforce and fortify."

..... .

No, General, no one is saying that you were wrong. I'm just making the point of how you consistently "request approval" for what has already been done or with full knowledge that a disapproval could not possibly reach you before the intended venture has become a *fait accompli*. At Vicksburg you were so right. You finally received Halleck's reply on May 17th. It ordered you, as you expected, to return to the river and join forces with Banks. The next day and you had Pemberton locked in his Vicksburg defenses.

..... .

Of course you ignored it --- and thoroughly baffled the poor staff officer who delivered it. He simply couldn't understand how you could not pay attention to a directive from the commanding general. The fact that you were standing in the rear of Vicksburg, its church spires in clear view, with the Rebel army fleeing toward the city in headlong retreat seems to have impressed him not at all. Orders are orders, after all. You, however, sensed that when the investment began the next day, Halleck would be appeased, and so he was. But did it ever occur to you that the order came from a higher authority than Halleck?

....?

What do I mean? Let's look at it. Remember what Lincoln wrote to you after the surrender: "When you got below, and took Port Gibson, Grand Gulf and vicinity, I thought you should go down the river and join Gen. Banks; and when you turned Northward East of the Big Black, I feared it was a mistake." The fact that he admits that you were right and that he was wrong doesn't change his original opinion --- it well may have been that Lincoln himself was directing Halleck to recall your army, ever think of that?

....

I hadn't imagined that it had occurred to you that way. I know that you always had a great deal of respect for the President. Why, General Grant, you seem to be a little pale. I realize that you didn't mind jousting with Halleck on occasion, but the President would have been a different matter, wouldn't it? But all's well that ends well, and when it was all over even McClernand was gone. Lincoln didn't make any comment about his unscheduled departure either. It could well have been that the President received a special communique from Dana about McClernand.

.. ... .

I can't help but agree with you. Everybody should have a spy like Dana around.

General, as your campaign is reviewed today, one hundred and twenty-five years later, it is still regarded as one of the finest in military history. Sherman was the first to applaud: "General Grant, I want to congratulate you on the success of your plan. And it's your plan, by heaven, and nobody else's. For nobody else believed in it." One military writer compared this campaign with Hannibal invading Italy, with Napoleon at Ulm and equal to the accomplishments of Caesar and Alexander.

Two recent military historians, the Dupuy's --- father and son --- may have summed up Grant at Vicksburg more accurately than *any* of the great writers: "Without in any way deprecating the magnificent troop leading of Lee and Jackson, the authors ... have often wondered why this exploit of General Grant receives, in general, so little attention from the same military historians who lay so much stress on the genius of the former two leaders. The Big Black River operation stands for all time as evidence of the audacity, vision and strategical ability of Grant. It is one of the great calculated risks of history."

... .

Yes, Sir, that's pretty heady stuff --- and I'll bet that you think that you deserve every word of it. This was your answer to the unjust newspaper men to whom you had given assurances that time would make things right. It also was a vindication of that feeling within yourself which immodestly proclaimed that you were the "Master of Predicaments."

... .

Oh, so you don't want to take all the credit. Of course it would have been impossible without the driving attitude of the troops and the leadership of your lieutenants. It's true that--- even if they doubted the wisdom of your plan --- they still fought like demons to make it work. That was a far cry from what would have happened in the East.

....

You'd better explain that one, General. You owe much of the idea for your plan to General Scott, General Van Dorn, and Mahan? Scott I can see --- you saw him cut loose from his supply lines in Mexico and win. Likewise Van Dorn --- his raid on Holly Springs taught you that the farms of Mississippi could provide sustenance for an army on the move. But what is this of Mahan --- he wrote on naval warfare, and at that it was twenty years after the war.

....

All right --- you got me. You were talking about the Admiral's father, Dennis Hart Mahan, who was an instructor at West Point when you were a cadet. "Rules," he lectured, "admit of many exceptions." and he would explain the value of speed in a military operation: "Speed is one of the chief characteristics of strategical marches, as it is of ordinary movements on the battlefield. No great success can be hoped for in war in which rapid movements do not enter as an element. Even the very elements of nature seem to array themselves against the slow and over-prudent general."

It seems strange, as we look back one hundred and twenty-five years to the Civil War, how few of your West Point colleagues --- regardless of class standing --- were able to translate the Mahan lectures into action.

... .

So, you felt that the Vicksburg campaign finally settled your debt with Sherman for leaving him in the lurch the previous December. It's true that Sherman had taken some newspaper flak for his failed attack at Chickasaw Bluffs, and as the encirclement was being completed and you both stood on the bluff, he did chide you for not being there when he needed you. But Sherman understood and he squared it all when he said, "Until this moment I never thought your expedition a success; I never could see the end clearly till now. But this is a campaign; this is a success if we never take the town."

It's odd, when you finally did take the town, Sherman wasn't there. He was at Jackson, again protecting the rear from attack. He wired congratulations and then he noted that Vicksburg was history --- the war must go on: "Already my orders are out to give one big '*HUZZA*' and sling the knapsacks for new fields."

... .

Yes, General, the new fields were hard to come by. No matter how you pleaded, you could not get Washington to come up with a plan of attack. Gettysburg was over and the Army of the Potomac was nursing its wounds in Virginia as it stared warily across the Rapidan River at a waiting Lee. Halleck, over your objections, spread your conquering Army of the Tennessee across the South as an army of occupation. He dismissed your idea for a movement against Mobile with the same disdain he had for your proposal against Fort Henry two years earlier.

... .

As you say, only Rosecrans and his Army of the Cumberland was on the move and even a strategical nonentity like Jefferson Davis could see that he had little to worry about from the Eastern and Western armies. So he reinforced Bragg in Tennessee with elements from the East and the West and, in September of 1863, Bragg was able to crush Rosecrans near Chattanooga, at a bloody battlefield known as Chickamauga Creek.

Within the month, you and Sherman knew what the new fields would be --- CHATTANOOGA.

CHAPTER SIX

"THE SPECTICLE (SIC) WAS GRAND BEYOND ANYTHING THAT HAS BEEN, OR IS LIKELY TO BE, SEEN ON THIS CONTINENT"

Chattanooga
(October 23-November 25, 1863)

SYNOPSIS: After Rosecrans' Army of the Cumberland lost to Bragg at Chickamauga, Lincoln was desperate. The brightening horizons which the President envisioned, after the Union victories at Gettysburg and Vicksburg were soon followed by the clearing of the Confederates from Tennessee, were suddenly obscured by ominous clouds. Bragg had the Army of the Cumberland penned in the valley around Chattanooga and it appeared that the Confederates would soon capture the army whole. To counter the Rebel advance, the Administration made several dramatic moves. Grant was ordered to send as many troops as he could to Rosecrans' relief and he ordered Sherman to start eastward. Even the Army of the Potomac made a contribution as General Hooker brought an augmented corps from Virginia to Chattanooga. Finally, Lincoln chose Grant to command this diverse army group.

Just a year earlier, Rosecrans served as an independent commander under Grant and despite a hard fought victory over General Van Dorn at Corinth, Mississippi, he earned Grant's wrath for failing to follow orders and achieving an even more overwhelming victory. When Secretary of War Stanton offered Grant either Rosecrans or George Thomas --- the same General Thomas with whom Grant had difficulties after Shiloh --- to command the besieged army, his unenthusiastic choice was Thomas.

Whether Grant was a great field general is a constantly debated topic. What may be said of him with certainty is that wherever he was things began to happen. The Army of the Cumberland had been nursing its wounds and slowly starving to death from day of the September 20th defeat until Grant's arrival on October 23rd. Then, in only a month, General W. F. (Baldy) Smith's plan to open a supply line was put into action, the army was refit and Grant was ready to assume the offensive.

Chattanooga was one of the few battlefields in the entire war where the commanding generals had a panoramic view of the unfolding drama. As the Union troops deployed to attack, they resembled an army about to march on a parade ground. This is the scene that Grant described to Congressman Washburne as a "grand specticle" (Grant's writing was and is universally praised for its correct syntax and direct prose; however, his spelling was atrociously imaginative). Chattanooga was also one of the few battles where it is still impossible to say exactly what happened and why. We only know that Grant had a plan; by mid-afternoon it was faltering; by evening, after the Army of the Cumberland made an impossible charge up a five hundred foot precipice, he had an overwhelming victory. He had also found General Philip Sheridan who would become his personal cutting edge in the final campaigns of the war.

Do you remember October of 1863, General? Charles A. Dana had been given a new assignment.

.... ?

He was sent by President Lincoln and Secretary of War Stanton to Chattanooga --- this time to spy on the recently defeated General Rosecrans. "The eyes of the government at the front," Lincoln called the ex-reporter and on October

16th, Dana gave his appraisal of the situation with the Army of the Cumberland: "The incapacity of the commander is astonishing. ... His imbecility appears to be contagious."

It seems, General Grant, that it was more than just a coincidence that on the same date a letter was dispatched to you which said: "You will receive herewith the orders of the President of the United States placing you in command of the Departments of the Ohio, Cumberland and the Tennessee." Secretary Stanton gave you the option of retaining Rosecrans in command of the Army of the Cumberland or replacing him with George Thomas, the "Rock of Chickamauga." Not surprisingly, Thomas got the job.

If nothing else, you were able to see first hand the power Charles Dana wielded within Lincoln's Administration. Dana arrived; Rosecrans was gone. It's a little frightening to think what he could have done to you had he believed the rumors which were making the rounds about you when he arrived at Vicksburg.

....

That's the way I see it, too. General U.S. Grant could very well have been sent packing to Galena.

... ...

So you were glad to see Rosecrans go. Obviously he wasn't one of your favorite generals --- a little surprising since he had served under you and actually won very handily against General Van Dorn at Corinth in October of 1862.

... .

So, you were still unhappy about his lackadaisical pursuit and his failure to follow your orders. Had he moved alertly, you say, and joined with General Ord's force as you had ordered, together they could have crushed Van Dorn's army --- the same army which caused you such embarrassment two months later when Colonel Murphy surrendered Holly Springs to Van Dorn. I guess the elephant never does forget.

.. ..

What do you mean that its hard to forget after being bitten twice?

... .

Oh, I see. You thought Rosecrans was out of your hair when he was given command of the Army of the Cumberland --- it saved you the trouble of relieving him --- but then he came back to haunt you during the six week siege of Vicksburg.

... .

You mean that he fought the battle of Stones River in December and then let his Army of the Cumberland sit idle for the next six months? No wonder you were furious; you wanted Halleck to get Rosey moving and stop Confederate Bragg from taking advantage of the lull by sending troops to your nemesis, Joe Johnston. Were you concerned that Johnston would become strong enough to break the Vicksburg siege before Pemberton surrendered?

... ...

Now I see what you mean, General. Johnston probably was not strong enough for his attack to have succeeded --- Sherman had little trouble chasing him away from Jackson after the Vicksburg surrender and Pemberton would have been of little help to him. His troops were too feeble after two months of siege to fight well. So the threat may have been more perceived than real. Nevertheless, as you say, the worry of your being squeezed between two Rebel armies was something that the already suffering Lincoln did not need in the summer of 1863.

I think that Halleck's wire describing Rosecrans' logic for sitting idle bothered you more than the threat from the Confederates. Poor old Rosey maintained that the rules of war posited that two decisive battles should not be fought at the same time. No wonder you were so critical of those generals who swore by the rules of war. Rosecrans finally did get moving toward Chattanooga in June of '63.

....

Yes it was just a few weeks before Pemberton surrendered. As you say, where was he when you really needed him?

... .

So you do give Rosecrans some credit for his ability once he got into action. You think that he was skillful in maneuvering Bragg out of Tennessee and in taking Chattanooga. But then came the battle which blew to pieces his logic of not fighting two battles simultaneously. This time Meade remained out of action after Gettysburg and your Army of the Tennessee was doing guard duty along the Mississippi River. Bragg's army then received reinforcements from every section of the Confederacy. Even Lee's Army of Northern Virginia sent Longstreet's Corps to Georgia and soon Bragg was able to match Rosecrans soldier for soldier. Rosecrans seemed unaware of what was happening under his very nose as he fanned his army out on a forty mile front to hunt down the foxy Bragg.

... .

I have to agree that Bragg was not an exceptional army commander. A fine officer and gentleman, but crusty and argumentative. If that describes Bragg, then he displayed all of his foibles as he prepared for this battle. The orders he issued were contradictory and confusing; however, his irascibility dissuaded his commanders from requesting clarification. As you said, the ensuing mix-ups kept Bragg from destroying the Army of the Cumberland one corps at a time. In the end Bragg had a victory, but he had to settle for less than a complete victory. Thomas's "*Rock*" stand and Gordon Granger's unordered march toward the sound of the guns allowed most of Rosecrans' army to find refuge in the valleys around Chattanooga.

....

Yes, Sir, that's where they waited and starved. It was a difficult time for this proud army...

... ...

General, it seems that you've always been too hard on this army --- ever since you encountered it when Buell arrived at Shiloh. Perhaps you can criticize Buell as a commander, but the men fought well on the second day at Shiloh and very bravely at Stones River.

.. ..

Well, you may not think that Stones River was all that great a fight, but it bears a remarkable resemblance to Shiloh. The Army of the Cumberland was pinned against the river but it never broke. Where Shiloh had Prentiss holding the "Hornet's Nest," Stones River had General Hazen's brigade saving the day at a hot spot called "Hell's Half Acre."

... .

Maybe you're right, perhaps Rosecrans should have pursued Bragg after the battle. But if we look at the close call he had had, I suspect Rosey was thinking as Sherman was eight months earlier when he said that you triumphant Yankees were happy to be rid of the Rebels under any circumstances.

... .

I know that you disagree, Sir. You're still bristling over how Rosecrans let Van Dorn escape and the way that the Cumberland generals treated you when you were in Halleck's dog house after Shiloh.

.. ..

Of course Phil Sheridan was an exception. You were disappointed when he left your Army of the Tennessee for a greener pasture in the Army of the Cumberland. But as

you've said so often, the Lord does work in mysterious ways
--- just a few weeks after you took command you were most
happy that "Little Phil" was a division commander in the Army
of the Cumberland.

Let me ask you something else, General. When Stanton
gave you the job, he offered either Thomas or Rosecrans as
Cumberland commander. If it had been left completely to
your discretion, of all of the available generals which one
would have been your first choice?

... .

After all these years, you say that you're still not sure, but
you think that it would have been Thomas after all. I find that
surprising. I thought that you may have chosen someone from
the Vicksburg campaign, possibly McPherson. You ranked
him second only to Sherman as a general.

... .

You don't think so. Hmm? You have a point. McPherson
would have been a relatively junior major-general from an
outside army --- he would have been regarded as an interloper
and no matter how good he was in the field he could not have
matched Thomas in knowing the situation, the enemy and the
officers and men of the Army of the Cumberland.

Another question, if I may? You met Rosecrans as he was
leaving Chattanooga to join McClellan, Buell, Frémont,
Pope, Stone, McDowell and the so many other Union
generals whom this war had burned out and devoured. What
was it like when you met?

.. ..

You mean that even as he was leaving Rosecrans couldn't
get squared away with you?

... .

I see. He explained this detailed and feasible plan for
righting the situation at Chattanooga, but to this day you take

him to task for not carrying it out. Weren't you somewhat nervous that Thomas may have suffered from the same lethargy? In reply to your first wire he said that, although they only had seven days rations, he and his men would hold the town until they starved.

.. ..?

I'll bet that's *not* what you wanted to hear. Your idea of success in war was not to stand pat and starve. Pemberton had done that at Vicksburg and he became a prisoner of war. You knew "Pap" Thomas, of course, but not well. He was ahead of you at West Point and you had that very cool relationship with him when Halleck took the field in Mississippi. Back then, you were still the titular commanding general of the Army of the Tennessee, but under Halleck's peculiar command arrangement, Thomas was actually running your army. To top it off, he virtually ignored you when you when you requested information about your own command.

... .

So that's when you toyed with the idea of resigning. You know, you never did give that part of your story the same emphasis which Sherman did. But you do admit to "toying" with the idea. Hmmm! Even that's a step forward.

At Chattanooga you met your West Point classmate, Joe Reynolds. He knew Thomas well. Reynolds told you: "Thomas [is] slow --- it's the god-a-mighty truth --- he *[is]* slow." In addition to his West Point nickname, "Pap," the troops called him "Old Slowtrot" because the pain from a back injury forced him to ride slowly. You always had your suspicions about the meticulous and slow Thomas, as we'll see when he faces General Hood at Nashville in December, 1864. But, General, particularly as Union generals go, Thomas was among the best and deserving of far more credit than you ever gave him.

....

You're right, General, let's get back to the Army of the Cumberland and its situation. The first impression you made on the Cumberlanders was a good one. They seemed to have been particularly surprised by your uncanny ability to understand their complex briefings, ask the right questions and penetrate right to the heart of intricate matters.

....

Even if, as you say, they explained the situation and the topography so plainly that you could visualize it easily, that's still quite an accomplishment. With the Tennessee River snaking through the ridges of the Appalachians, I'd find it difficult to follow with or without maps.

But as the story unfolded you didn't need a map to understand just how desperate the Army's situation was. There was only a week's rations for the men, forage for the horses was gone --- thousands of animals were already dead --- and there was sufficient ammunition for just one day of battle. Little wonder that Sherman's first words to you were, "General Grant, why you are besieged."

....

I guess you did have only one answer, "It is too true." But the situation was soon to turn about. It was done quickly. You arrived at Headquarters on the 23d of October, issued orders to get the "cracker line" plan working on the 24th and by November 1st the troops were receiving full rations. In just.....

....

You have a point, General. We're throwing terms like "cracker line" around as though everyone understands the meaning. I think we'll first have to describe the fix in which the Army of the Cumberland found itself.

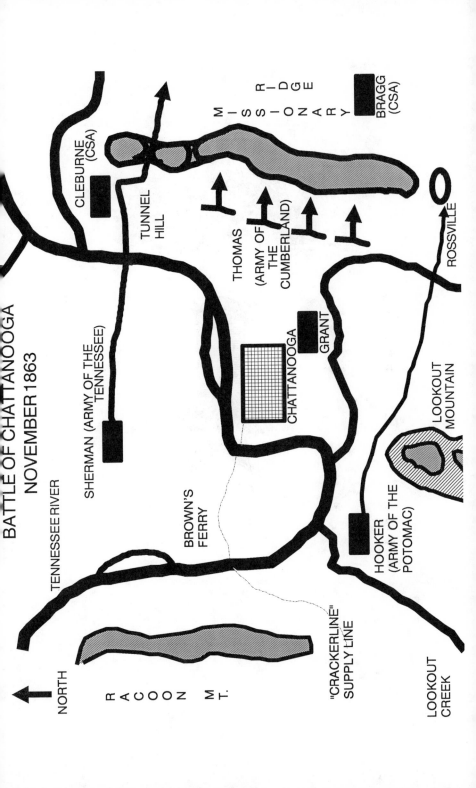

BATTLE OF CHATTANOOGA
NOVEMBER 1863

NORTH

TENNESSEE RIVER

RACOON MT.

SHERMAN (ARMY OF THE TENNESSEE)

BROWN'S FERRY

"CRACKERLINE" SUPPLY LINE

LOOKOUT CREEK

CLEBURNE (CSA)

TUNNEL HILL

THOMAS (ARMY OF THE CUMBERLAND)

CHATTANOOGA

GRANT

HOOKER (ARMY OF THE POTOMAC)

LOOKOUT MOUNTAIN

MISSIONARY RIDGE

BRAGG (CSA)

ROSSVILLE

And the first thing I'm going to do, Sir, is to invite our readers to look at the map.

As we said earlier, after the Battle of Chickamauga, Rosecrans pulled his defeated divisions into the valleys around the town of Chattanooga. The town is located in a hairpin bend of the Tennessee River and at the end of a valley which is bounded to the west by Lookout Mountain and to the south and east by Missionary Ridge. The ridge slants from the southwest to the northeast until it peters out east of town in a series of small hills which blend into the south bank of the river. Except for the well entrenched break south of town between Lookout Mountain and Missionary Ridge, Rebel artillery on the high ground dominated all approaches to the city.

... .

I didn't forget the north side, Sir. In that sector the terrain was also an aide to besiegers. When you came to Chattanooga, the ride from the end of the railroad line at Bridgeport took your light-traveling party two days to cover a distance of some sixty-five miles. The roads in that area were nothing more than farm paths wandering through the foothills of the Great Smoky Mountains. The quartermaster's mule trains took at least five days to cover the distance --- and that was in good weather. That meant that the wagons carried far more forage for the animals than supplies for the beleaguered army.

....

Yes, General, I remember what you wrote, "The roads were strewn with the debris of broken wagons and the carcasses of thousands of starved mules and horses." Nevertheless, only a trickle of supplies ever reached the Army of the Cumberland and guards had to be staked out at the animal feeding stations to fend off the hungry soldiers.

....?

Right! Let's get to the "cracker line." It was the brainchild of "Baldy" Smith. His plan called for a small offensive against Bragg's left which gave the Union forces control of a portion of the river a few miles west of Chattanooga and just beyond the range of the rebel artillery. (Here's the place on the map --- Brown's Ferry.) Once accomplished, he built a pontoon bridge across the Tennessee River and cut a new road across the spit of land formed by the curl in the river north of Chattanooga. A second bridge into the north side of town made the connection complete. The distance which supplies then had to be moved by wagon was reduced to only fifteen miles and by the end of October, food, ammunition, and clothing were flowing into the besieged city.

... .

Oh, "cracker line," I almost forgot. When the food arrived, a major part of it was that crusty cracker-like bread the men called "hardtack," hence the name "*Cracker Line.*" Feel better now, Sir? Anyway, in three weeks the army was completely resupplied, Sherman was moving his Army of the Tennessee into position to fight, and Hooker, who had brought a corps from the quiescent Army of the Potomac, was poised to pounce.

... .

That's right, General, in addition to what was happening at Chattanooga, Washington was in a tizzy about Knoxville. General Burnside had a small force there and after Chick-amauga, Jefferson Davis sent Longstreet north to pry Burnside out of the town. As you said, "The President, the Secretary of War, and General Halleck were in an agony of suspense" about Burnside's situation.

....

I have to say that that does seem peculiar. It appears that everyone, including yourself, seemed to be concerned about Burnside's welfare with the exception of Burnside. He had a form of cracker line going himself and felt reasonably secure. This general feeling of anxiety finally had an impact on the post-battle situation at Chattanooga, however, since you felt it necessary to break off the pursuit of Bragg's army and send Sherman directly to Knoxville. But let's not get too far ahead of ourselves. I just wanted to make the point that Knoxville was very much on your mind.

....

So, on the 24th of November, you felt ready to attack Bragg. Prior to the 24th, there had been several false starts as a fuming Sherman struggled to get his army into attack position. You planned that Sherman would be your powerful left hook while Hooker on your right was a maneuvering force to keep Bragg distracted and confused. Thomas's Army of the Cumberland was under orders to be ready in the center should Bragg weaken his Missionary Ridge ranks to counter the attacks on his flanks.

....

Yes, Sir, it was a fine plan, but translating it into action was a different story. Sherman, climbing the northeast bluffs of Missionary Ridge, found both the terrain and the Confederates too much to handle. The division of the Irish-born Confederate, Pat Cleburne, stopped the mighty Army of the Tennessee dead in its tracks. However, the plan still had enough flexibility to work. Hooker had cleared a jump-off point on Lookout Mountain on the 24th and early on the 25th you expected to see him sweep into Bragg's rear forcing the Confederate leader to withdraw units from Sherman's front. Hooker, however, was stopped by Chattanooga Creek for four hours while his men built a bridge.

....

So, you thought that the whole plan was coming unglued. Did you know that even Sherman was accusing you of having gone daft for urging him to continue his stymied advance? Then came the great mystery!

Thomas's army, to the soldiers chagrin, had been virtually out of the battle. Don't you think that this proud bunch of fighters wanted nothing more than to avenge Chickamauga Creek?

....

I know that they had their job to do, General, but I think that you are missing the point. They were lined up in the lengthening shadows of Missionary Ridge while your Vicksburg veterans and the "fancy-pants" Easterners were doing the fighting. It was bad enough that they needed rescuing, but then to have someone else fight the battle against their tormentors must have been hard to stomach. You know, General, it also may be that neither they nor Thomas had a clear idea of just what they were supposed to do.

....

There you go getting testy again, General. You say that they should have known --- it was all in the orders you had sent to Thomas. Well, let's look at the orders since everyone seems to interpret them differently: "I have instructed General Sherman to advance as soon as it is light in the morning, and your attack, which will be simultaneous, will be in cooperation. Your command will either carry the rifle pits and ridge directly in front of them, or move to the left as the presence of the enemy may require."

....

Yes, Sir, that does seem clear enough. Thomas will go with Sherman at first light. Now let's look at how you explained it: "Hooker was off bright and early [but] he was detained four hours crossing Chattanooga Creek ... his reaching Bragg's flank and extending across it was to be the signal for Thomas's assault of the ridge." Now which is it? Attack at dawn with Sherman or wait until Hooker appeared on Bragg's flank? The truth is that nobody seems to know any more. The battle has become so befuddled with myths and legends --- stories about a lunar eclipse which addled men's minds, of Lookout Mountain's "Battle above the Clouds" during which the Almighty lifted the cloud cover to allow an unfurling "Old Glory" to be bathed in radiant beams and then a miraculous charge by the subpar Army of the Cumberland. Even your final order for Thomas to advance is clouded in some sort of lunacy. You were certain that you had seen Bragg send more units to oppose Sherman and --- if we assume that Hooker was to have been the catalyst to swing Thomas into action --- you could wait no longer for Hooker. You ordered Thomas forward.

.... ?

The lunacy, my good General, is that neither Bragg nor his staff ever have admitted that reinforcements had been sent from the Rebel center and left. What's more, the Rebel order books confirm what they say --- very few troops were moved toward the northeastern knob at all.

....

Look, General, it really mattered little that all of the irritants which the gods foist on mere mortals were raining on the environs of Tennessee that day --- what did matter was at 2 P.M. on the 25th of November 1863, your whole cavalcade was at a standstill. It was last resort time --- move the Army of the Cumberland forward just enough to get Bragg's attention. Maybe, just maybe, Bragg would concentrate at his center at the expense of his flanks.

... .

Yes, Sir, it was worth a try. As the French Marshal Foch said at a crucial moment in his war: "My center is giving way, my right is pushed back ... I will attack." Surprisingly it worked for him and it worked for you. The Army of the Cumberland moved into the rifle pits at the base of the ridge as ordered, reformed on their own and, in an ultimate display of lunacy, swept up and over the ridge driving the Confederate soldiers before them.

General, you've had time to think about the battle. Do you have any clearer idea of what actually happened to send the Army of the Cumberland on such a wild spree?

... .

So, you believe that the momentum was psychological --- the reverse of when a trained army suddenly flees in panic. You think that with the rescuing troops stymied, the Army of the Cumberland had something to prove. The line soldiers resented being blamed for the defeat at Chickamauga when they believed that the fault belonged squarely on the shoulders of the generals.

... ...

I know that you weren't at Chickamauga, General, and I'm not trying to read too much into your remarks. But you have spoken at length to those who were there. After all, General Wood was your West Point classmate. He must have given you some ideas to explain what happened.

... ...

You believe, then, that the biggest psychological block held over from Chickamauga was actually in General Wood's division. That was the outfit which Rosecrans had ordered out of the front lines just before Longstreet came pouring through their gap. Yes, they felt that the whole fault for the debacle was being heaped on them despite the fact that Wood was obeying a direct order from the commanding general. So, it seems to you that the most embarrassed division in this embarrassed Army of the Cumberland was Wood's Division. When they were given a chance to prove their mettle, they simply went a little overboard.

... .

Your idea then is that it was some form of mass hysteria which propelled them up the hill and into the trenches of their former antagonists. But why did Bragg's veterans break and run? Could it have been that that eclipse of the moon on the night of the 24th had the world just a little out of whack?

... .

You don't want to blame the moon then. It sounded good --- after all the Rebels were closer to the moon than the Federals. You really believe that they just weren't ready for what happened. I know that they thought the Union army was rolling out for a review when it actually was deploying to attack. The Union Army had to be lining up for a parade, they surmised. No sane commander would order an attack on their impregnable position. You even described it to Congressman Washburne (with your own unique spelling) as, "The specticle [sic] was grand beyond anything that has been, or is likely to be, on this continent. It is the first battlefield I have ever seen where a plan could be followed from one place, the whole field being within one view." The Confederates may have seen it the same way, and suddenly the paraders were among them --- with gleaming bayonets. At any rate, the siege was over, no matter how it happened.

... ...

That's right, Sir, it wasn't all over yet. You still had to contend with Knoxville --- and Lincoln wasn't about to let you forget it. With the President's laurels came a thorn: "Well done. Many thanks to all. *REMEMBER BURNSIDE!*"

... .

No he couldn't have been clearer and you didn't need any further prompting. Before the fighting had even ended on November 25th, you had Sherman on the march.

....

It is too bad that Washington didn't have a better feel for Burnside's plight. The move to rescue him, which really didn't require a big rush, prevented an aggressive pursuit of Bragg's fleeing troops. You may have missed the opportunity to remove the Army of Tennessee from the board entirely.

... .

Yes I had almost forgotten --- that incident was particularly unfortunate. Sheridan's division had blocked Bragg's right wing from retreating from Missionary Ridge. However, when Sheridan called for help, Corps Commander Granger decided that his sleep was more important than a battle.

... .

So that ended Granger's already slim chance for any serious command.

....

Yes Sir, you win some and you lose some. You found out about Granger before he was ever put in a position of responsibility, but you got a very wrong impression of "Baldy" Smith. You fought for his promotion to major-general and later you thought that he would offset Butler's ineptitude with the Army of the James. Not so, as we'll see. On the other hand, Sheridan proved in the Shenandoah campaign and in 1865 that what you saw at Chattanooga was right on the mark.

But let's remember, General, of all the key players at Chattanooga --- Thomas, Sherman, Smith, Sheridan, Granger, Hooker --- the one whose world was changed most by the dramatic victory was yours. Vicksburg may have been a more significant achievement, but Pemberton's surrender had been somewhat overshadowed by Lee's defeat at Gettysburg. The victory at Chattanooga was all yours. Rawlins probably summed up the impact best when he wrote to his fiancé that "Grant's 'star' is still on the ascendant and will continue to be while it lightens the patriot's path."

.. ... .

No, General, this time I don't believe that Rawlins over-stated the case. Actually he was prophetic. In three months Congress would revive the rank of lieutenant-general and Lincoln would give the job to you --- Commander-in-Chief of the Union Armies.

... .

That's right, General, a new era was about to begin in the war. No longer would the Federal forces pull, as you described them, like a "balky team." One would not sit idle while another fought a reinforced enemy. Henceforth, the Union armies would move in concert.

....

So, you think that it's time to move east. Let's do it.

CHAPTER SEVEN

"THAT MAY ALL BE WELL, BUT BOBBY LEE IS WAITING JUST ACROSS THE RAPIDAN."

Virginia
(May-June 1864)

SYNOPSIS: As 1863 came to a close, Lincoln reviewed his situation: 1) If the war were not over before election day, the voters would determine the outcome. 2) They had to be made to feel that the end was imminent or they would elect a president who would agree to Southern independence. 3) General Halleck had proven to be a cipher as Commander-in-Chief. A new and dynamic commander was needed to lead the Union Armies to victory. 4) Lincoln had gone through dozens of generals since the beginning of the war and Meade, the latest commander in the East, had proved to be offensively unimaginative since his defensive victory at Gettysburg in July. The only general in whom Lincoln had confidence was Ulysses Grant. Lincoln decided that he would bet the country's future on this grubby Mid-westerner whom most of the slick West Pointers despised.

Lincoln may have been convinced that Grant was the man, but the generals who had been dazzled by Lee's successes were less confident. They were quick to murmur to Grant's staff that the new Commander-in-Chief may have enjoyed success against Confederate mediocrity out West, but Lee was a different breed of cat and he was waiting close by to pounce on the hapless Grant. To counter their reluctance to accept Grant and to make it clear who was to be in charge, Lincoln promoted Grant to lieutenant-general. Grant then shared center stage with George Washington in the annals of American history and, moreover, he clearly outranked the plethora of major-generals who saturated the Union Army.

With the exception of General Banks's political show of force against Mexico's Maximillian, Grant assumed control of every facet of the Federal Army's operations --- from minor skirmishes with the Indians to the massive offensives against Generals Lee and Joseph Johnston. He assigned the trustworthy General Sherman to command in the the Western theater, giving him control of the Armies of the Tennessee (McPherson commanding), Cumberland (Thomas commanding) and Ohio (Schofield commanding). Sherman's orders directed him to move against Atlanta and Johnston's army.

Meade retained command of the Army of the Potomac as it moved against Lee, but Grant would be within shouting distance to assure that the army moved as he wanted it to move. In addition to these drives into the heart of the Confederacy, Grant planned two less striking but nevertheless important advances. One was the movement into Virginia's Shenandoah Valley which was to have denied Lee access to both his breadbasket region and his favorite route into the North. The second was an amphibious movement up the James River to the outskirts of Richmond.

In the Shenandoah, first General Franz Sigel then General Donald Hunter failed miserably. In just six weeks the Valley was a wide-open avenue to the gates of Washington. The move on Richmond fared no better. Competent leadership by General Ben Butler, a Massachusetts Democrat of the McClernand stripe and Lincoln's desperately needed political ally, may have made this one of the most important military ventures of the war. When the Army of the James disembarked fifteen miles south of Richmond, fewer than four thousand Rebels stood between the thirty-three thousand man Union army and the Confederate capital. Grant had counted on Butler's corps commanders, W.

F. Smith (who had performed so well at Chattanooga) and the battle tested Quincy Gillmore, to provide Butler with sound military advice. Instead the three took to bickering among themselves and rather than sharing the glory for taking Richmond, they negotiated the Army of the James onto a spit of land in the James River called Bermuda Hundred where the Confederates penned it in and took it out of the war.

The far-flung armies rolled on May 4th, 1864. The Army of the Potomac crashed into that desolate wasteland called the Wilderness where General Hooker had come to grief just one year before. The Army of the Potomac and Lee's Army of Northern Virginia fought virtually every day for five weeks and made hallowed shrines of such woebegone places as Spottsylvania*, North Anna River, and Cold Harbor. They finally reached the banks of the James River, both armies badly bloodied but Lee still a defiant and potent foe. Grant looked at Lee's impenetrable trenches and the great river on his flank and made another of those momentous decisions which characterized his leadership.

* The modern spelling is Spotsylvania; however, the maps and reports of the Civil War use Spottsylvania.

Good morning, General Grant. Welcome back to Virginia. There's been a lot of changes over the past one hundred and twenty-five years. Are you able to tell where we are?

....

That's the place all right, but you don't have to be so irritable about it. You knew that we'd have to come to Cold Harbor eventually if we were going to tell your whole story. And let's face it, rightly or wrongly, Cold Harbor is universally regarded as the low point of your entire military career --- and well it should be.

....?

No, I didn't mean to include your bad scene with Colonel Buchanan on the West Coast. I was talking about the Civil War years. But I can't blame you for not wanting ever to see this place again. It's such a gloomy hole now --- it must have been a lot worse then. Remember what you wrote in your *MEMOIRS* about this battle? It was one of the few times that you ever looked back unhappily: "I always regretted that the last assault at Cold Harbor was ever made.... At Cold Harbor no advantage whatever was gained to compensate for the heavy loss we sustained." You wrote that line almost twenty years to the day after the battle and your readers can easily see that the carnage at Cold Harbor still haunted you.

.... ?

I'll tell you why we've come here, General. To tell the truth, I have always wondered why this battle was fought. You had hammered against Lee's trenches at Spottsylvania and when you saw him dug-in at the North Anna River you decided that only Union casualties would result from attacking him there. Then you came to Cold Harbor and sent half your army against his entrenched troops.

Had you been able to launch an all-out attack on the morning of June 2nd as you originally planned, there was an excellent chance of success. But waiting twenty-four hours while the "King of Spades" had his troops working their shovels seems to have been pure folly.

Do you think that, with one hundred years to think about it, you may be able to explain more fully just what happened here? After all....

....

What do you mean that you don't want to deal with Cold Harbor as an isolated case?

....

That's true enough, General. Cold Harbor was part of a campaign --- the campaign which began when the Army of the Potomac crossed the Rapidan River on May 4th and moved into the Wilderness.

So, you want to start with the Wilderness battle and follow the two armies step by step for the month it took to reach Cold Harbor.
....

Well if you say that we can't understand this battlefield unless we understand the events which led up to it, then I guess that's what we'll do. As it happens the battlefields are largely intact --- Wilderness, Spottsylvania, North Anna River, they're all there.

At each stop the intricate network of trenches which the two armies dug are surprisingly well preserved. Neither people nor earth have forgotten what went on in the Virginia countryside over a century ago.

If that's what you want, then let's head up to the Rapidan River and start at the beginning.
.... ?

The way we whisk you around I can't blame you for feeling like Scrooge being carted about by the spirits. Now we are on Clark's Summit. I don't think that you've ever been here before. This is the place where Lee and his corps commanders had their very last battle conference. It took place on May 1st, and from this vantage point the Rebel generals could see the bustling activity in the Union army's camps. They knew the signs well --- the conclusive battle of the war was only a few days away.

As he watched the Army of the Potomac prepare, Lee believed that if he could drive Meade's Army back across the Rapidan as he he had sent McClellan, Burnside, Pope, and Hooker reeling north, the South would likely win both the war and its independence. Across the river, you, the Grant of Donelson, Vicksburg and Chattanooga, were mounting an offensive which the tortured Lincoln believed was the last opportunity to preserve the Union.

In a few months the political parties would select their candidates for the election of 1864. Both sides fully expected that the Democratic convention would propose a peace platform. If you, General Grant, could not demonstrate that victory would come soon, the war weary northern voters would likely choose to end the bloody conflict --- that is if Lincoln had not abandoned the effort first.

....

Yes, General, it certainly is a spectacular view. From here, Lee's scouts could see every move your army made and they would wig-wag the information to Lee when the Army of the Potomac began to roll. Only then would Lee know whether you had chosen to slide the Union troops to the west of the Army of Northern Virgina or move through the Wilderness.

On May 1st, Lee felt that it would be the Wilderness --- he knew as well as you that a Union army faced great difficulties keeping supply lines open away from the Union Navy controlled rivers. On May 4th, he had his answer and he ordered his scattered army to move cautiously toward the Wilderness.

....

Yes, General, we know that you had hoped to get the Army of the Potomac through the Wilderness before Lee could collect his dispersed corps and move against you. Your plan called for the army to move rapidly toward the open country beyond that tangled mass of underbrush, thickets, and second growth trees. In this country, advantages of manpower and artillery were for naught. Unfortunately, the Army of the Potomac did not have the highly trained reflexes required for rapid movement when circumstances were ideal. To move one hundred thousand men and a sixty-five mile long wagon train over roads which were little more than cow paths with any semblance of celerity was not within the army's capability. As it happened, General Ewell, under orders not to bring on a major fight, moved his corps forward for what was to have been a reconnaissance in force --- only to have his men collide with the Union's V Corps as they groped their way through the gloomy jungle. Lee may have preferred to wait for Longstreet's Corps, but suddenly the battle was on.

... .

You were *very* willing to oblige Lee if he chose to fight you in the Wilderness. You had that one significant piece of intelligence which, you knew, gave the Union force a distinct advantage. Longstreet's Corps, based at Gordonsville some 35 miles away, would not arrive at the battle scene for at least a day --- for twenty-four hours the Army of the Potomac would be fighting only two-thirds of Lee's army. The fight, moreover, fit into your strategic battle plan for the three primary Union armies: Strike at the Rebel armies everywhere. Your instructions to General Meade and his Army of the Potomac were perfectly clear: "Lee's army will be your objective point. Whereever Lee goes, there you will go also." Lee was in the Wilderness. The Army of the Potomac would fight him there.

... ...

That's right, General, virtually the same instructions did go to Sherman: "You I propose to move against Johnston's army, to break it up and to get into the interior of the enemy's country as far as you can..." That's a good point. The Union armies were no longer going to be dispersed in gathering and protecting real estate as Halleck had done. The target was the Rebel armies --- the lifeblood of the Confederacy. If they were no longer effective fighting forces, the territory could be occupied at will. We'll have more to say about your strategy later, right now I'm anxious to get back to Cold Harbor to find out what really went on there.

The Wilderness is probably better described as a struggle rather than a battle. It resembled the groping and grappling of two blind wrestlers, not the fancy geometric patterns outlined in the tactics manuals. In the smoky haze and thick woods, both sides squandered opportunities for a decisive, if not complete, victory. Delays, cautiousness, command inefficiencies, and some plain bad luck prevented the Army of the Potomac from crushing Hill's Corps before Longstreet arrived on the battlefield. Lee's opportunity came when General Gordon discovered that the Union army's right flank was wide open. Unfortunately for the Rebel cause, it took Gordon all day to get his attack proposal through the Confederate chain of command. He finally hit Sedgwick's VI Corps on the evening of May 6th, and the spectre of Jackson's flank attack against Hooker in this same area just a year earlier mesmerized the Union generals.

....

That's just the point I wanted to make, General. You had heard nothing from these generals but *Lee, Lee, Lee* since you had arrived in the East. Fortunately for the preservation of the Union, you did not share this overpowering fear of General Lee and his army. As we've already discussed, you felt that he was mortal. "That may all be well," they said as you briefed them on your plans, "but Bobby Lee is waiting just across the Rapidan." Now they were telling you that Lee was upon you and you'd best have the Army of the Potomac beat a hasty retreat toward Washington.

....

We know, General, that you had no intentions of retreating --- ever. The bridges across the Rapidan had been removed already. The Army of the Potomac was in Bobby Lee's back yard to stay and your comments to the prophets of doom left little to their imaginations. "Oh, I am heartily tired of hearing about what Lee is going to do," you bellowed as they desperately urged retreat. "Some of you always seem to think he is suddenly going to turn a double somersault and land in our rear and on both flanks at the same time. Go back to your commands and try to think what we are going to do ourselves, instead of what Lee is going to do."

Your opinion of Lee never seemed to match that of your colleagues in the Army of the Potomac. As a matter of fact, you frequently listed General Joe Johnston's military ability as superior to Lee's.

... .

You're right, General, let's not get into that discussion now. We have a war going on at the moment and we'll have plenty of time to get into personalities after the battles are over.

What I would like to know is how you felt after the battle in the Wilderness. You lost about seventeen thousand men, and no matter how you try to minimize the anxieties brought on by General Gordon's flank attack, you did see an entire corps of Meade's army being saved from potential destruction only by the onset of night.

... ...

General, I beg to disagree --- things may have been *that* bad. I know that your aide Horace Porter commented that you felt everything was under control and that you simply went to sleep. However, General James Wilson, a former member of your staff, and in 1864 the commander of a cavalry division, stated that you withdrew to your tent and "... gave vent to [your] feelings." Wilson knew you well, possibly better than any of your assistants with the exception of Rawlins. The fact is that even if Wilson erred and you had not wept in your tent, his belief is an indication of the terrible strain that he felt you were under. Now, what's your opinion of the situation *after* the battle?

... .

You were satisfied? Satisfied that you had a victory? That doesn't say very much. What do you mean by "satisfied?"

... .

Very well, I must admit that you and the Army of the Potomac had several notable successes that week. Over one hundred thousand men, fifty thousand horses and four thousand wagons had crossed over a formidable stream un-molested. As you said, in single file the wagon train alone would have stretched the entire sixty-five miles to Richmond. You certainly had every reason to be satisfied with the cross-ing and happy that Lee had not attacked during the maneuver. So what's next?

... .

Of course --- next came the battle itself which you described as the most desperate fighting ever witnessed on this con-tinent. When it was over, both armies had been mauled, with the larger Union army somewhat getting the worst of it.

... .

Yes, I do agree that the Army of the Potomac was still intact as a fighting force nor had Lee been able to send it scurrying northward. It's also true that, although the Union losses were severe, Lee's losses (over eleven thousand by some estimates) had a more devastating impact on his smaller force. After the Wilderness, Lee was never again able to commit the Army of Northern Virginia to a full-scale offensive movement.

... .

As you say, Sir, the National troops must have felt that they had achieved a great victory once they realized that from the

Wilderness they were heading south and were not mounting another "great skedaddle."

....

Tell me about it, General. You had to order that the troops stop their lusty cheers so the enemy would not be alerted to the move. Was that when you felt that the men sensed that they had just passed through the beginning of the end?

... ...

I have to agree, Sir. The senior officers in the Army of the Potomac saw something new to them as well. You were well aware of what had happened in almost every battle in the East. One commander after another seemed to lose touch with his situation once the fighting began. I would say that only Meade at Gettysburg kept even a semblance of control of things as that battle raged relentlessly toward its conclusion.

In the other battles the commanders faltered. McClellan on the Peninsula had been mesmerized into believing that he faced a foe three times its actual size; Burnside at Fredericksburg couldn't picture the battlefield into which he had sent his army and let one wing be slaughtered while the other remained dormant. Both Pope and Hooker seemed to drift aimlessly as Lee split his forces and mauled them.

It's probably very true that your imperturbability and your ability to react quickly to Lee's counterstrokes was totally new to the the Eastern generals. They may have grumbled that the army's losses were too high or that the Army of the Potomac should have withdrawn to refit before fighting again, but the comments about what Bobby Lee might do seemed to fade from then on.

What you said to your staff on May 7th appears, then, to be an accurate portrayal of your feelings about the Wilderness: "We cannot call the engagement a positive victory but the enemy have only twice actually reached our lines in their many attacks and have not gained a single advantage. This will enable me to carry out my intention of moving to the left, and compelling the enemy to fight in a more open country and outside of their breastworks." Now, how come the breastworks were a problem here but not at Cold Harbor, General?

....

OK, we'll discuss it at Cold Harbor then. Meanwhile, the terror of the Wilderness had ended --- the terror of Spottsylvania was about to begin. Before we leave the Wilderness, General, is there anything else you'd like to say about the battle?

....

You want to mention Colonel Mosby and his raiders? What do you have to say about those renegades?

... .

I see, you don't regard Mosby and his troopers the same as the marauders and night-riders who seemed to roam everywhere in Virginia. Now that you mention it, I do remember that you had met Mosby after the war and were very favorably impressed with him. So, you still think that Mosby contributed significantly toward preventing the Army of the Potomac from crushing at least a part of the Army of Northern Virginia in the Wilderness. Except for the fact that Mosby's existence virtually ruled out the western route to Richmond, how do you conclude that he had such an enormous impact on the battle?

... .

Yes, Sir, I think everyone understands the problem, as long as the Union army was away from a major river, it had to be supplied overland --- usually by a combination of railroad and wagon train. In Virginia, therefore, no western movement as long as Mosby was around. I'd say that it was very much like Mississippi during the Vicksburg campaign.

....

So that's why your guidance to Meade indicated that he could marshal his entire army for the move across the Rapidan. The Army of the Potomac had been guarding the rails, but on May 4th, Burnside's IX Corps took over the job from Manassas south. The result? You were short a twenty-five thousand-man Corps when Hancock attacked Lee on the morning of May 6th.

You finally have to admit then, the raids Van Dorn and Bedford Forrest conducted against your Mississippi supply lines in late '62 were still on your mind. Mosby was the Bedford Forrest of the East. He was every bit as effective at evading Union cavalry and he had the same annoying habit of wiping out rear echelon supply depots. Mosby actually had fewer men than the average regiment, yet there he was, able to keep an entire corps pinned down for over a day just to protect lines of communication.

....

But on the afternoon of May 4th, with the Army of the Potomac and its trains across the Rapidan, you felt that you could surrender the Orange and Alexandria Railroad to Mosby's cavalry. Your orders went to Burnside to move his corps forward with all deliberate haste. You wanted him in place to support Hancock's attack against the isolated A.P. Hill.

....

That's right, you couldn't fault Burnside for the rapid movement of his corps into the Wilderness area --- he could have been mistaken for Stonewall Jackson. But then, on the morning of the 6th, he was the same old Burnside again. It then took him the entire morning and most of the afternoon to get into the fray.

....

I know that you still think that the Wilderness is a difficult area in which to move a corps and you'll get few disagreements. But Burnside, like your old buddy Rosecrans, was not born for speed. The end result was that Hancock's men gave Hill's a drubbing, but did not deliver the crippling blow which you had hoped to see.

....

I must admit that your statement makes sense when you explain it that way. Mosby's tiny band kept an entire Union corps out of the Battle of the Wilderness at what might have been the most critical hours. So there it was, the old nursery rhyme coming alive: "For the want of a nail the battle was lost." Fortunately, the remaining dire consequences didn't come to pass --- just another couple of hundred thousand casualties on both sides before the end finally did come. As some sage once said, "Dying is a soldier's lot." Perhaps it is true --- some things which we say should not have been were simply meant to be.

As we move toward Spottsylvania, General, do you have any similar observations about unusual circumstances playing a major role?

....

I never thought that I'd hear you say that, General --- you really believe that luck was a major factor in the outcome of the Battle of Spottsylvania. It's not like you to use the term "Luck" so casually --- or should I say "causally."

....

That's true, you did say once that luck could influence the outcome of a battle, but you always added that you did not

believe that luck could determine the outcome of a campaign. But what is this luck which was so important at Spottsylvania?
... .

All right, let's discuss a little of the background first. General John B. Gordon, the same General Gordon who led the attack against the Union right on the evening of May 6th, later told you that he listened as Lee studied the options after the fighting in the Wilderness had subsided. A Union retreat, as Hooker had done the year before, was a possibility, but, in Lee's mind, not likely. He thought that you were as aware as he that if the Army of the Potomac crossed the Rapidan again it was tantamount to giving the South its independence. You were Lincoln's last hope --- if he couldn't trump Lee with you in command then Old Abe had no more cards to play.

Even less likely was the possibility of renewing the fight in the Wilderness where the South had all the advantages. Lee believed that you would move. To General Gordon, he said, "Grant will renew the fight in the morning at Spottsylvania Court House."

... .

So that's where luck came into play. Lee ordered Longstreet's Corps (commanded by Richard Anderson after Longstreet had been wounded) to be in Spottsylvania on the morning of the 8th. Anderson, intending to stop enroute, started his men late on the 7th. However, the woods were still aflame in the aftermath of the gory battle and the marching Rebels could not find a suitable bivouac area. Thus, Longstreet's Corps marched through the night, arriving at Spottsylvania shortly before dawn on the 8th.

A division of Union cavalry had been holding the town awaiting the arrival of the Union's V Corps to secure the place. Anderson, however, arrived first and the Union cavalry was unable to hold the village against an infantry corps. With

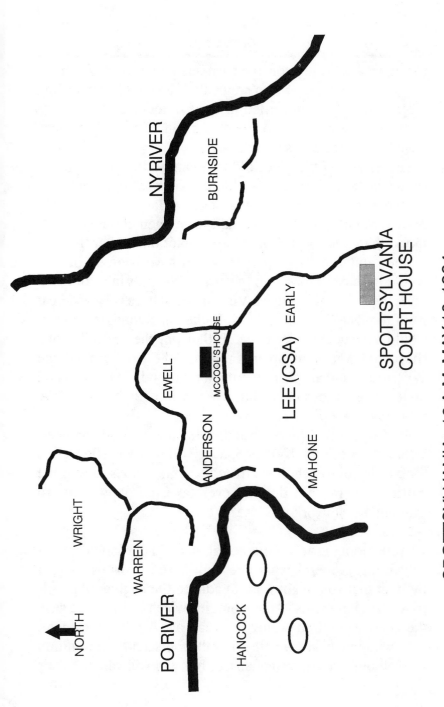

SPOTTSYLVANIA - 10 A.M. MAY 10, 1864

the town his, Anderson then wheeled to thwart V Corps' thrust. The matter of who controlled the vital Spottsylvania crossroads had been settled to the Confederates advantage with less than an hour to spare. As you said, the issue may have been settled by simple chance.

Yes, Sir, that little piece of luck changed the entire course of the campaign and the two bloody weeks of fighting in the trenches around Spottsylvania began. Had the Union held Spottsylvania, your troops would have been closer to Richmond than Lee. That would have meant that either the race to the capital and its defenses would have been on or Lee would have been forced to the attack. With its inferior numbers, the Army of Northern Virginia could have very well beat itself to pieces in such assaults. In the Richmond defenses, it would have been under siege. Either way the possibility of a shortened war went up in smoke in the fires around the Wilderness and another seventeen thousand Union men and at least ten thousand Confederates joined the sacrificial procession.

In the battle which ensued, Lee, the master engineer, retained his title as "King of Spades." I know you had a good look at his entrenchments from the Union lines during the battle, General, but did you ever take the opportunity to examine his network up close?

....

Even if looking at war memorials and old battlefields is not your thing, General, what Lee built here is worth seeing. I thought that you might want to admire the engineering. Almost all of it remains --- the scourging which you and Lee gave the soil one hundred twenty-five years ago is still very evident. The wooden braces in the bombproofs and ammunition storage buildings have collapsed, but you still can see their

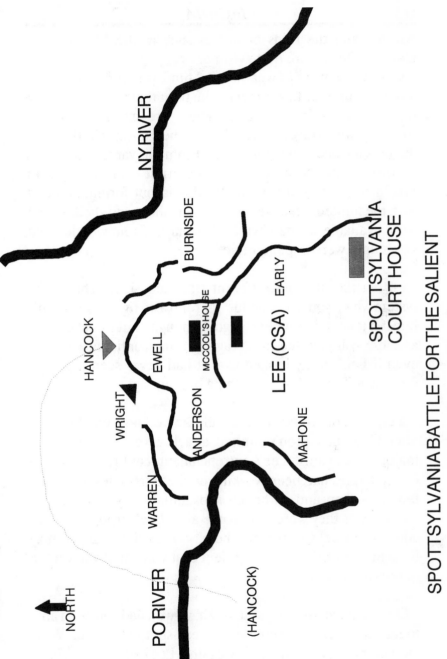

SPOTTSYLVANIA BATTLE FOR THE SALIENT
MAY 12, 1864

outlines and the ruins of homes such as the McCool and Harrison houses are quite visible.

Despite the wear of weather and time, you don't have to be a skilled observer to appreciate the treat that Lee had waiting for your attacking soldiers. There are multiple lines of trenches with traverses leading to the concentric fields of dugouts terraced up the hillsides. From this vantage point his sharpshooters had a field day. The armies which fought in World War I would have found this layout formidable and with the limited effectiveness of the artillery and shells which were available to the Civil War armies, it's no wonder that Lee's lines were impenetrable.

... ..

I'll bet that it looks different from this side. This is the system which you wrote about: "I propose to fight it out on this line if it takes all summer." A good thought, but trenches such as these will give the most rag-tag army confidence --- and even if Lee's army looked as if it had never seen a parade ground, militarily it was anything but rag-tag.

... ...

Yes, General, you wrote that "all summer" note on May 11th, after General Upton's limited attack gave promise that a major move against Lee's entrenchments could succeed. The Confederates had been working on these trenches for only a few days then and, although substantial, they were not as awesome as they were to become after Lee's troops had two additional weeks to perfect them. So, on the 11th you may have had reason to feel confident that you could win on the Spottsylvania line.

....

Oh, you mean that you still may have won had you been able to maneuver Lee into creating a weak spot in the line. What kind of maneuvers did you try against Lee?

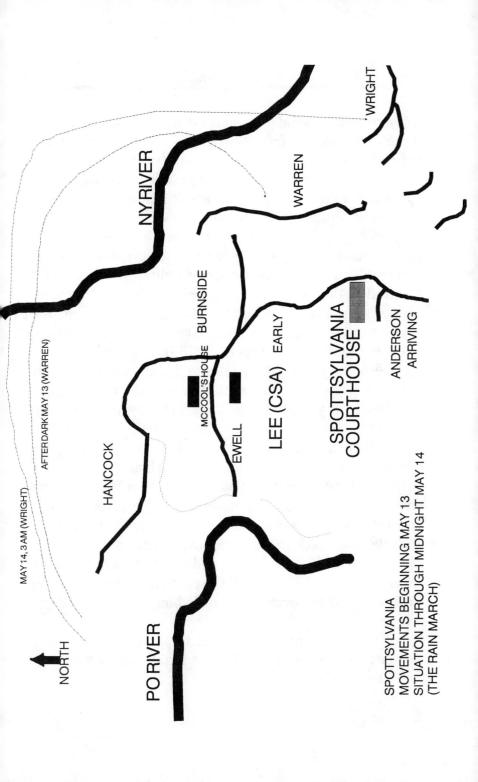

NORTH

MAY 14, 3 AM (WRIGHT)

AFTER DARK MAY 13 (WARREN)

PO RIVER

NY RIVER

WRIGHT

WARREN

HANCOCK

BURNSIDE

MCCOOL'S HOUSE

EWELL

LEE (CSA)   EARLY

SPOTTSYLVANIA
COURT HOUSE

ANDERSON
ARRIVING

SPOTTSYLVANIA
MOVEMENTS BEGINNING MAY 13
SITUATION THROUGH MIDNIGHT MAY 14
(THE RAIN MARCH)

... .

Good grief, General, I was only asking a simple question ---
there's no reason to bite my head off. It's a good thing that
you never did swear. Anyway, I see what your driving at. You
say that on six of the twelve days the armies were at Spottsylvania you tried to get Lee to commit himself and create a
weakpoint somewhere in his lines.

For instance, the first two days both armies were constantly
on the move as they skirmished for position. Then came
Hancock's move from your extreme right to your center for
an attack at the apex of the great inverted "V" Lee's trenches
formed. The Union referred to the area as "the Salient," the
Confederates called it the "Mule Shoe." After the battle it
became known to both sides as the "Bloody Angle."

General, do you mind if I refer to the maps to see exactly
what was happening? I know that the events are still fixed in
your mind and you don't need them, but some of us aren't so
fortunate.

The move succeeded in confusing Lee and, in what was a
rarity, he made a mistake. He misread Hancock's shift as a
major withdrawal so he pulled his artillery from the salient
should a quick pursuit be necessary. The error was discovered, but the Confederates compounded it by trying to
rush the guns back to the Mule Shoe. They arrived simultaneously with Hancock's men and twenty of the guns were
taken. Along with the guns, II Corps captured four thousand
men, some eight percent of the dwindling Army of Northern
Virginia.

All right, General, the Army of the Potomac did have a
degree of success against the Salient, but the men didn't crack
Lee's line.

... .

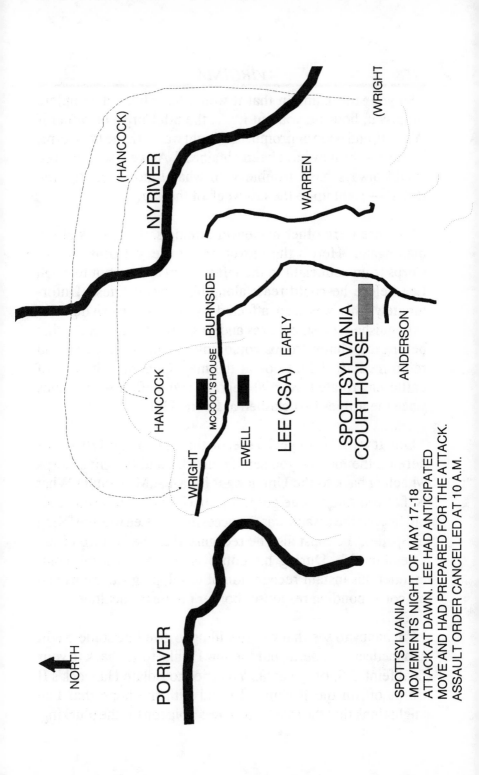

NORTH

PO RIVER

NY RIVER

(HANCOCK)

(WRIGHT

WARREN

BURNSIDE

HANCOCK

WRIGHT

MCCOOL'S HOUSE

EWELL

LEE (CSA)

EARLY

ANDERSON

SPOTTSYLVANIA
COURT HOUSE

SPOTTSYLVANIA
MOVEMENTS NIGHT OF MAY 17-18
ATTACK AT DAWN. LEE HAD ANTICIPATED
MOVE AND HAD PREPARED FOR THE ATTACK.
ASSAULT ORDER CANCELLED AT 10 A.M.

So you still maintain that it would have been a complete success if, how did you put it? "... the 5th Corps, or rather if Warren, had been as prompt as Wright was with the 6th Corps, better results may have been obtained." As we'll see, Warren would always have trouble with what Lincoln called "the slows" --- right up to the last week of the war.

.. .. .

So there were other maneuver attempts. Let's look at the map again. Here's the movement of the V Corps and VI Corps from your right to the left flank in an attempt to catch Lee before he could react along his interior lines. Unfortunately, this was also affected by luck --- a driving rain extinguished the signal fires and so slowed the marchers that before the Union troops could unleash an assault, Lee had reinforced *his* right. Look at the map, General. The line of battle has rotated over 90 degrees and shifted seven miles since the armies first clashed at Laurel Hill.

... ...

Oh! It wasn't over yet? I see, on the night of the 17th --- it's here on the map --- you sent Hancock's and Wright's Corps wheeling back to the Union right for a 4 A.M. assault. What is that you said? "Lee got troops back in time to protect his old line, so the assault was unsuccessful." If Lee was the "King of Spades," he must also be recognized as the "Prince of the Chessboard." During his entire career as an army commander, his instant recognition of developing situations and his corresponding responses border on the miraculous.

... .

I'm happy to see that you're willing to give Lee some credit as a tactician, General, but for now I'd like to get back to your final feint at Spottsylvania. You tried to isolate Hancock's II Corps off on the Richmond Road with the hope that Lee might think that the lonely corps was a pigeon for the plucking.

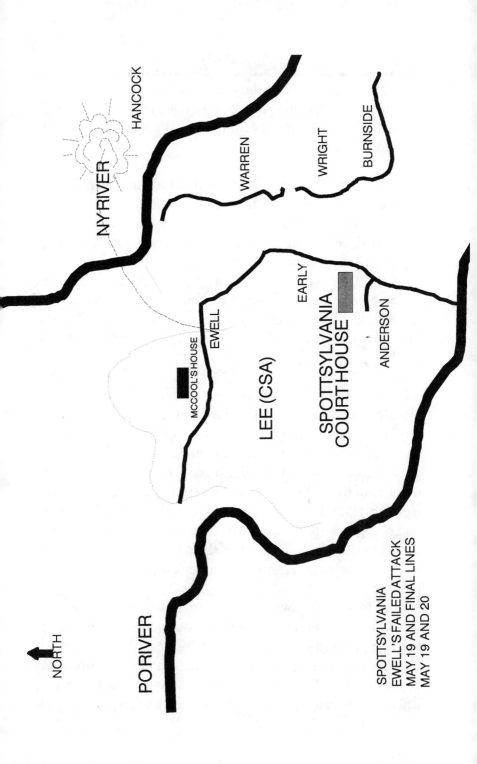

NORTH

PO RIVER

NY RIVER

HANCOCK

WARREN

WRIGHT

BURNSIDE

McCOOL'S HOUSE

EWELL

LEE (CSA)

EARLY

SPOTTSYLVANIA
COURT HOUSE

ANDERSON

SPOTTSYLVANIA
EWELL'S FAILED ATTACK
MAY 19 AND FINAL LINES
MAY 19 AND 20

Lee didn't take the bait, however, and on May 20th, twelve days after Warren and Anderson first sparred at Laurel Hill, the Army of the Potomac withdrew and began moving toward the North Anna River.

.. ... .

I understand, Sir. You don't want me to miss the point that you offered Lee an opportunity to attack an isolated corps and he refused even to make a feint. You maintain that this event, combined with the action at the North Anna, tended to shape the decisions you made later in the campaign.

All right, Sir, we shall see. In my opinion nothing happened at the North Anna. Three of the four Union Corps crossed the River, the two armies stared at each other for a few days and then you sent the Army of the Potomac racing for Cold Harbor.

.. ... .

I agree, General, that the young men who died at the Chesterfield Bridge and Jericho Ford wouldn't care to hear me say that nothing happened at the North Anna --- but Lee was sick with ptomaine poisoning, Longstreet was still incapacitated from his Wilderness wound, A.P. Hill, commander of the Third Corps, had just returned to active service from an extended illness and was not yet up to a hard campaign, and Ewell was about to succumb to a sickness which would virtually take him out of the war. Let's be honest, the Army of Northern Virginia was practically leaderless and out of action.

If we look at the overall situation, however, we'll see that the Army of the Potomac wasn't in much better shape. Warren and Wright had crossed the river by Lee's left flank while Hancock's II Corps had crossed to the east along the Telegraph Road. (By the way, the road is still there, only we call it U.S. Route 1 now). But Burnside's IX Corps, which was

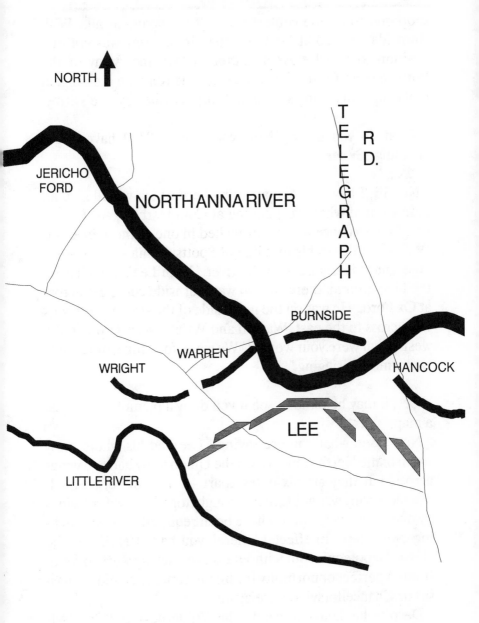

supposed to be the center, couldn't get across at all. With Burnside stymied at Ox Ford, the Union army was *not* in a position to attack. As a matter of fact, the Army of the Potomac was, for the first time since the Rapidan crossing, in real danger of having an isolated corps crushed by Lee's army.

....

What do you mean, "Now you've got it?" I haven't got anything, General.

....

No, Sir, I haven't seen anything here which would give an indication of what was pending at Cold Harbor. All I see is that Lee was once again entrenched in one of those inverted "Vs" --- similar to his first line at Spottsylvania --- except his nose guard is squarely on the river. With Lee's trenches on the high ground, there was no way Burnside could get across at Ox Ford. He was on the north side of the stream, Hancock was across to the east, Warren and Wright were across to the west. What were your words? "We were, for a time, practically two armies besieging."

.. ..?

Yes, it may help me to see if you drew a picture --- at least a map.

Now I see what you are saying. Lee had his whole army south of the North Anna River; the Union army had two wings across, but they are six miles apart --- Lee in between. If Meade's army was going to be brought together, two crossings by one of the wings would have been required --- Lee watching every step. In effect, General, you had offered Lee the classic Napoleonic split without his even having worked for it. It was a perfect opportunity for him to repeat Second Manassas or Chancellorsville once again.

Despite his heavy losses in the Wilderness and Spottsylvania, Lee at this point was not particularly undermanned. He had been receiving reinforcements --- you claimed fifteen thousand, others put the number closer to ten thousand --- so his army was close to the numbers which he had when the campaign began. The only question was: When would Lee attack?

.. ..

You're quite correct, General, Lee didn't attack. Now we know why. He was too sick to get out of his tent and his corps commanders weren't in much better shape. With the army leaderless, an offensive move was out of the question.

... .

No, General, you didn't know that then. You thought that Lee's failure to act meant that his army had lost its spark.

.... ?

Yes, Sir, I've read it. On May 26th you reported to General Halleck: "Lee's army is really whipped. The prisoners we now take show it, and the action of his army shows it unmistakably." You then added that you felt success over Lee was already assured. General, tell me, could you have been suffering from a severe case of overconfidence?

... ...

You *do* believe that you were overconfident. As you say, the prisoners may have been saying what they thought you wanted to hear. That's not unknown --- or could it have been that you were hearing only what you wanted to hear? That's not unknown either. No matter how you slice it though, Lee's army was far from being down for the count and if you put those veterans behind earthworks they were still as dangerous as jungle cats.

....

Now you want to go to Cold Harbor --- the stage is set, you say, to intelligently discuss what happened there. You'll see that the terrain and landmarks have not changed all that much over the years. Some new buildings, but overall I think you'll recognize our route. Ready to whisk?

Here we are. If you like we can trace those devilish trenches for the more than five miles from Bethesda Church to the Chickahominy River.

.... ?

No, we don't have to walk the whole five miles --- just enough to give us some idea of how extensive the lines were.

Now, we noted that you seemed overconfident as you moved from the North Anna, but you still hadn't ruled out a sudden thrust by Lee. Let's look at May 30th, the day that "Baldy" Smith and his XVIII Corps from the Army of the James joined the Army of the Potomac for this supposedly final smash at Lee's army. As Smith was marching to join Meade, you felt that his lonely and disorganized corps would have been the perfect target for one of Lee's rapier forays. You warned Meade: "It is not improbable that the enemy, being aware of Smith's movements, will be feeling to get on our left flank for the purpose of cutting him off, or by a dash to crush him and get back before we are aware of it."

.... ?

Why did I bring up this cautionary note? I think it's important to understand that, despite your confident statements about the Army of Northern Virginia, you still had a lot of respect for Lee and the threat that his army posed.

....

Oh, you wanted it to be a polite reminder to Meade that Lee was still dangerous, but more importantly, should he make a foray, you wanted the Army of the Potomac prepared both to stop it and to smash the Rebels.

... .

Yes, Lee *was still* Lee, and you were very aware that any misstep could bring him on you like a tiger. With this in mind, it does seem that --- particularly with your armies deep in enemy territory --- your desire to end the war in the East was boiling over. You had held Lee at bay for a month, but as long as he and his army existed, there was always the danger that the old magician could pull another military miracle out of his hat and upset your entire strategic plan. I think the term the pundits would use today to describe your attitude is "guarded optimism."

... .

Come on, General, there is more than just an *element* of truth in the statement. I think that it was a major factor in your wanting to end the campaign against Lee north of the James River. You knew that the crossing of the James could be done; however, you also knew that such a monumental maneuver was fraught with danger. You seemed to be thinking: "Why do it? If we can beat Lee at Cold Harbor and push on into Richmond it won't be necessary."

... .

So you thought that a victory at Cold Harbor would have changed the tactical scene in the East. Lee would have been forced into the trenches and he would have needed every troop he could have gotten his hands on to protect Richmond. Butler, then, may have been able to burst out of his self imposed Bermuda Hundred prison, Hunter easily could have controlled the Shenandoah Valley and the Confederate position in the East would have become untenable --- the war may have been over.

An outstanding concept, but once again it fell apart in the execution. First let's look at the lay of the land --- something which the officers of the Army of the Potomac should have done with more diligence. Lee had his army stretched from the Chickahominy River almost six miles to Totopotomoy Creek. To cover such a front, his line had to be thinned almost to the breaking point. However, he did have the advantage of great flank protection --- no turning movement was possible. Lee, moreover, the consummate engineer, made up for his lack of numbers by weaving the trench line so carefully that every flaw in the terrain had been exploited and the positioning provided interlocking fields of fire. Lee's disadvantage was the length of the line --- he had not a soldier in reserve. General, have you ever heard the story of the discussion between Lee and the Confederate official, John Reagan, just before the battle?

....

No? I didn't think that you had. As the Army of the Potomac troops massed for the attack, Reagan was appalled. He asked Lee about his reserve in case of a breakthrough. "Not a regiment," Lee replied, "if I shorten my lines to provide a reserve, he will turn me. If I weaken my lines to provide a reserve, he will break them." That's how close a call it was for Lee. Once again that river boat gambler was betting everything on the next roll of the dice. He obviously understood the danger; however, Lee apparently believed that a calculated risk was better than the alternative --- a siege.

The Richmond defenses were carefully devised engineering marvels. They were far stronger than field fortifications and Lee's army easily could have held the perimeter against a million men. But to Lee, the trenches meant "siege" --- his army would never again have an opportunity to seize the initiative. As he had said to General Early, the end would be only a matter of time.

....

I understand that General, a siege was not to your liking either. Siege meant death to thousands of soldiers --- not from bullets but from disease. You had seen such results at Vicksburg, and, although Virginia was not as tropical as Mississippi, summer in the swamps around Richmond was not a healthy place for New Englanders or Westerners.

One at a time you added the factors: In your mind, Lee's army was whipped; also, you had no more room for maneuver north of the James; you further believed that more men would die from a siege than from one last all-out attack. Moreover, with Hunter in control of the Valley and Butler free to operate against Petersburg, the siege would probably not last long. It added to one conclusion: "Attack." The only thing that you overlooked was Lee's skill in building field fortifications over-night and the tenacity of the Army of Northern Virginia.

... .. .

All right, Sir, let's look at it from your point of view. You could see that Lee's trenches were formidable, but for a change they were in a straight line --- something you had not seen at either Spottsylvania or the North Anna. Lee would not have the advantage of quickly moving troops along interior lines to bolster a weak point. A breakthrough, or even a serious dent, meant trouble for Lee.

... .

No, Sir, I haven't forgotten that the Federal attacks on the evening of June 1st were very successful. There was every indication that a quick follow-up on the morning of the 2nd could have penetrated the Confederate line. The problem, as we both know, was that the attack didn't come on the 2nd as ordered. I'm sure you remember that your headquarters gave General Smith erroneous marching instructions when he dis-embarked at White House. He finally arrived at Cold Harbor, but without his ammunition trains. Meade turned the air blue as he damned him for bothering to come at all. To add to the confusion, the engineers led Hancock's Corps into a dead end shortcut and were able to "shorten" a nine mile march to sixteen.

At the time the assault had been scheduled, 4:30 A.M., Hancock's men were still miles from the jump-off point. Rescheduled for 4 o'clock in the afternoon, the weary II corps was still not ready to move out. Then came the most inexplicable blunder of the campaign --- the order to delay the attack until the morning of the 3nd of June --- you gave Lee a full twenty-four hours to prepare his special greetings.

An assault at dawn of June 2nd had an excellent chance to succeed. The Army of Northern Virginia, with its veteran corps commanders virtually incapacitated, was not the crisp organization of the year before. It's true that the men had been digging all night, but the Rebel positions were not yet stabilized. By the 3rd, they were so dug-in that senior commanders were not needed --- Lee's troopers knew their jobs. Worse yet, no senior officer on the Federal side seemed to recognize what the Army of Northern Virginia had accomplished during the twenty-four hour delay.

The works were awesome. Journalist Charles Page described them in detail at the time: "They are intricate, zig-zagged lines within lines, lines protecting flanks of lines, lines built to enfilade an opposing line ... a maze ... laid out with some definite design either of defense or offense."

....

Yes, it is a grim story. You sent them in on that June 3nd and no battle in the war --- not Malvern hill, Pickett's Charge, your assault at Vicksburg, nor Fredericksburg --- dropped so many soldiers so quickly. In twenty minutes, some 7,000 men were lying in the Virginia dust either dead or wounded. The other attacks may have resulted in more casualties, but not in so short a time span. It took the machine gun of World War I to replicate what Lee had accomplished at Cold Harbor.

.. ..

General, I know that you weren't proud of what happened here. You wrote that you had always regretted the assault. You may have been able to rationalize the Wilderness and Spottsylvania into victories --- and with some justification. But Cold Harbor was a defeat for the whole Union chain of command. If, as we said before, getting killed was the expected fate of a soldier, then Cold Harbor served its purpose.

General Grant, no matter how much I read about this battle or how many times I have walked around these trenches, I still come to the conclusion that you were so convinced that Lee's army was whipped and that on the 3rd of June the Army of the Potomac was so superior to the Army of Northern Virginia, nothing could dampen your enthusiasm. The fact that Lee was so ill at the North Anna River that even in that perfect tactical situation he was unable to strike a blow had you believing that his army was held together by a thread.

....

Oh I agree with you, General. It is very unfair of us with over a hundred years to think about it and with the chance to see the cards both sides were holding, for us to pass judgment on the decisions you and Lee had to make on the spot. Your opinion of Lee's army was based on the facts as you saw them, but it does seem that you stretched the significance of those facts --- the lack of offensive effort and the opinions of prisoners --- to fit your preconceived mold.

Cold Harbor was over...

....

Yes, Sir, I think that we've both seen enough of this place. It's time to get to that last river crossing as we head towards Petersburg.

CHAPTER EIGHT

"I THINK IT IS PRETTY WELL TO GET ACROSS A GREAT RIVER AND COME UP HERE AND ATTACK LEE IN THE REAR BEFORE HE IS READY FOR US."

Petersburg
(June 1864-April 1865)

SYNOPSIS: On June 17th, Grant had the Army of the Potomac across the James River and Butler's Army of the James was bursting out of its "corked bottle." There's no doubt that the Commander-in-Chief felt the glow of victory sweep over him. Here he was in Lee's back yard and Lee was not yet aware that the Union army had abandoned its Cold Harbor lines. In a rare display of euphoria, he announced to his staff that he was happy to be in a position to attack Lee before the master was ready. His joy, however, was premature. The attack which he expected to bring such dramatic results failed; a subsequent foray following the explosion of eight thousand pounds of powder under the Confederate trench lines also came to naught. The two armies settled down to a siege as the Union forces tried to pinch off the remaining railroads which supplied the Confederate capital.

In the other theaters the Lieutenant-General's plans were faring no better. After General Hunter's poorly orchestrated campaign left the Shenandoah Valley devoid of Union troops, Lee once again took advantage of the open avenue and sent General Jubal Early's corps to the very outskirts of Washington. The threat to the capital was more perceived than real and soon the Army of the Potomac's VI Corps had Early retreating to the cover of the Blue Ridge Mountains. Grant had had enough of the Valley --- he sent his most ferocious general, Philip Sheridan, to the Shenandoah with orders to "... eat out Virginia clean and clear so that a crow flying over would have to carry its own provender."

In Georgia, Sherman was progressing slowly as the canny Joe Johnston gave ground grudgingly. In August of 1864, Lincoln reviewed the bidding and wrote to his cabinet that the situation was such that he had all but given up hope of being reelected in November. Fortunately, within a month the universal stranglehold which Grant had placed on the Confederacy began to take effect. Sherman went crashing into Atlanta, Sheridan finally did corner Early in the Shenandoah, and Admiral Farragut neutralized Mobile. The Eastern armies were still locked in a deathgrip, but signs of decay were appearing throughout the Confederacy. It was Grant's strategic plan of applying pressure across the South which won Lincoln's election for him.

There's the James River, General Grant; we're looking at it from Jordan's Point, a few miles down river from what used to be City Point.

.... ?

The town is called Hopewell now, General, and City Point is a section of the new town. That big bridge crosses the James from Jordan's Point to Harrison's Landing. Recognize it now? If you look west you can see the old City point area where you had your headquarters for nine months. Looking down river, around that point of land, you can see where the great pontoon bridge was built --- the bridge which the Army of the Potomac used to cross over for the attack on Petersburg.

As you gazed at this river in 1864, it was the one time in the entire campaign against Lee that you actually felt unbridled optimism. For six weeks you had the Army of the Potomac on the move in an attempt to get around Lee's army. The master always seemed to be a step ahead of you and Meade.

There were many reasons for the failures --- bad weather, sheer incompetence and let's not forget Lee's skill. However, in departing Cold Harbor so cleanly, you finally had stolen a march on him. and for that one shining moment you felt that there was no way Beauregard's scratch force could keep Smith's and Hancock's combined corps out of Petersburg.

....

I'm glad you brought that up, General. I was wondering what was so important about Petersburg. It was only a tiny hamlet sitting twenty miles south of Richmond, yet it was an objective for the Army of the James in May of '64 and you were celebrating that the combined Armies of the Potomac and the James were about to take the town. You claimed that Petersburg was the key which opened the lock to Richmond and Lee's army. Why?

....

Of course, I should have guessed --- railroads. With one exception, all of the railroads used to supply Richmond and Lee's army passed through Petersburg. If Petersburg fell, the remaining line not only would have been insufficient to keep the capital supplied, but Union cavalry could have kept it torn up. So this was the *BIG* opportunity --- a chance to force Lee to abandon Richmond with its massive defensive network and give Meade the chance to hit the Army of Northern Virginia while Lee attempted to shift his army further south.

....

All right, General, you say that this was what you had been working toward throughout the whole campaign. Now what does that mean. Your instructions to Meade indicated that he was to have followed Lee's army to the death; now you are saying that the capture of Petersburg had been in your plans from the very beginning. Will General Grant's real war plan please stand up!

....

You're actually trying to tell me that you had always known that Lee would be a tough nut to crack and if the Army of the Potomac wasn't able to break him north of the James the job would have to be be done south of the river.

....

Yes, I suppose I do look a little puzzled --- nonplused as you call it. I must admit that I overlooked the message which you sent on May 26th which started the pontoons and bridging equipment moving into position on the James. I suppose that I was too wrapped up in what was going on along the North Anna and tracking your "Lee's Army is whipped" message to Halleck to notice. Now you're saying that even as you were announcing Lee's demise, you were anticipating a move toward Petersburg.

....

Perhaps you're right, General. It well may be time to take a look at your overall strategy for this campaign. Right now it seems to be changing every day.

....

Good heavens, General Grant, there you go waking the dead again. In no way did I mean to imply that you never had a strategic plan and I've certainly been around long enough to realize that once a campaign begins the best plan will have to change to fit the unfolding situation. I was just asking that you explain it a little more clearly --- I may not be the only one who has been confused by what happened between Spottsylvania and Petersburg.

....

All right, let's start at the beginning. We've already discussed why you chose the Wilderness route rather than moving through Orange and Gordonsville. You also ruled out a major campaign up the Peninsula as McClellan had done. Such a plan would have been an open invitation to Lee to send the Army of Northern Virginia on another northern invasion. Stanton also would have recognized this possibility and very likely would have won his argument that you maintain a substantial part of the Union Army between Lee and the capital. I see your point but not everyone agreed with you. Look what General Martin McMahon of VI Corps later wrote as he declared the overland campaign (and particularly Cold Harbor) a disaster:

Cold Harbor was a discouraging fight in every particular...Two years before this same army [under McClellan]had been placed much nearer Richmond with comparatively little loss. ... But the plan of an overland march to Richmond, while protected navigable waters within our control led to the very door, was fully tried between the 3d of May and the 15th of June and had failed.

....

I can see that the General's comments haven't changed your mind. You still maintain that a movement around Lee's right flank through the Wilderness was the only practical alternative.

....

General, I know that you never swore nor used profanity, but you just came as close as anyone I've ever heard of going beyond "doggone it." I *do* get your point. You still believe that critics like McMahon are dupes who refuse to look at the totality of operations in the Spring of '64 rather than the Army of the Potomac alone. You're still incensed that the only thing that the people in the East could see was the struggle between Lee and McClellan's old army.

Lee had to be defeated or at least controlled, you say, but these experts never really understood that the war was between two governments and not a rivalry between two armies.

....

Thank you, maybe I *am* catching on to your thinking, but I would still like to go over your plan step by step.

Am I right to say that your first objective was to use Richmond as the anvil on which you intended to beat the Confederacy into submission? For the Confederacy to continue the war --- much less win the war --- the Rebels believed that Richmond had to be held at all costs. Richmond was the Confederacy's, and particularly Jefferson Davis's, symbol of independence. The loss of the capital would certainly have killed the very slim chance that the European powers might recognize the Confederate government. Without Richmond, Davis believed, the Confederacy would have ceased to exist. The capital, therefore, had to be protected at all costs --- and as long as Meade's army threatened the city, Lee would have to stay to oppose him.

... .

Yes, I can see it all start to fall into place now. What you really wanted was not only pressure on Richmond but for the Union to pressure the Confederacy on all fronts. So that's why your initial orders to Meade and Sherman directed them to make the opposing Confederate armies their objective points. As long as the two major Union armies stayed in close contact with their adversaries each Confederate army would have to fight for its own survival and would not be able to detach units to provide assistance in another theater.

... .

Yes, Sir, we did see how Lee was able to detach Longstreet's Corps to aid Bragg at Chickamauga when Meade remained idle after Gettysburg. You were going to assure that such excursions would not happen on your watch.

... .

Well, are you going to be magnanimous toward the self-proclaimed military masters such as General McMahon and

forgive them for not seeing the connection between operations conducted by the Army of the Potomac and Sherman's
forces some 600 miles away?

..· · ·

I thought that was too good to be true. You still fault them
for not at least seeing what was happening under their noses
with Butler and his Army of the James.

... .. ·.. ·

You're right. If McMahon wanted to take a boat ride to the
gates of Richmond all he had to do was ride with the Army of
the James. Meade's objective point was Lee's army --- your
orders of April 2nd to Butler made his objective Richmond:

*Lee's army and Richmond being the greater objects towards
which our attention must be directed in the next campaign, it is
desirable to unite all the force we can against them. The necessity of covering Washington with the Army of the Potomac and
of covering your Department with your army, makes it impossible to unite these forces at the beginning of any move. I
propose, therefore, what comes nearest this of anything that
seems practicable: The Army of the Potomac will act from its
present base, Lee's army being the objective point. You ... will
operate on the south side of the James River, Richmond being
your objective point ... and there is to be co-operation between
your force and the Army of the Potomac. Then should the
enemy be forced into his intrenchments in Richmond, the Army
of the Potomac will follow, and by means of transports the two
armies would become a unit.*

I have to say that when we look at it all together, it's quite
clear what you intended in the opening stages of your campaign. Meade's army would lock onto Lee and hold him well
north of Richmond while Butler and his thirty-three
thousand, virtually unopposed, acted as the maneuvering wing
against the capital.

Sherman later wrote that he saw your 1864 strategy as a *three* pronged plan of attack. He was your right wing, Meade the center and Butler the left. But your thinking didn't stop there, did it?

....

I see. As the armies were about to move you envisioned several possibilities. As Butler and his Army of the James threatened Richmond, Lee may have retreated from the area of the Rapidan River into the Richmond defenses immediately. Once he was ensconced in the trench network he could easily have fended off both Union armies. You hoped that Meade would be able to strike a crippling blow against Lee while he was marching south, mauling the Army of Northern Virginia so badly that it would not have remained an effective fighting force.

The next possibility you foresaw was Butler failing in his drive to capture Richmond and Petersburg while Lee safely maneuvered his army into the Richmond defenses. Then, as you wrote to Butler, the two Union armies would join in a siege.

In your third scenario, Richmond would fall to Butler as Lee abandons the capital and, in a last ditch effort to continue the war, marches to unite with the southernmost Confederates. Your counter plan called for the combined armies to overwhelm Lee's retreating forces before they could reach General Johnston and his Army of Tennessee.

The final script was the one which was finally played out: Butler would be ineffective and floundering in his march against the Richmond- Petersburg area. Then, with hardly a glance toward Richmond, Lee would stand his ground in such unlikely places as the Wilderness, Spottsylvania, North Anna and Cold Harbor. As a result, the Army of the Potomac would be forced to slug its way south to link-up with the Army of the James.

... ...

No, General, I didn't forget about Sigel's small army in the Shenandoah Valley. I thought that Sigel had slipped *your* mind.

... .

Understand, Sir. As you say, you may be old but you're not that old --- so I have no choice but to agree that your memory is still as sharp as a tack. Back to Sigel --- his three purposes in life were simply to stay in existence in the Valley, be a distraction to Lee, and to prevent Lee from sending Jackson-like sweeps down the Shenandoah to threaten Washington. However, the Confederates under General John Breckenridge, with reinforcements from the Virginia Military Institute cadet corps, needed only two weeks to drive Sigel completely out of the Valley.

....

So you replaced Sigel with Hunter, the same Hunter who had first replaced Frémont in the West. He immediately drove to Lynchburg and appeared to have a successful campaign under way. However, as the Army of the Potomac and the Army of Northern Virginia eyed each other warily from their Cold Harbor trenches, Lee was able to pry Jubal Early loose and "Old Jube," along with General Breckenridge, pushed Hunter clear out of the state of Virginia.

... .

Yes, you certainly were enraged when Hunter went barreling straight west into West Virginia. In effect, he took his army out of the war for almost three weeks. That's when Early pushed across the Potomac, brushed past General Lew Wallace's scratch force at the Monocacy River and moved into the outskirts of Washington itself.

... .

Oh it's well known that you expected little from Sigel or from Butler for that matter. After all, both were political generals --- the Union's answer to the Floyd-Pillow combination you met at Fort Donelson.

... .

I understand that the two West Point trained corps commanders assigned to Butler's army were supposed to provide sound military advice; unfortunately "Baldy" Smith, your old friend from Chattanooga and his colleague Quincy Gillmore were were unable or unwilling to work with Butler. While they fretted and fumed, the Confederate Beauregard was able to push Butler onto Bermuda Hundred, a peninsula between the James and Appomattox Rivers, and lock him in there "... as if he were in a bottle firmly corked."

... .

That's right, two weeks into the campaign and the two armies which you had hoped would have distracted the Confederates from focusing all of their attention on the Army of the Potomac had been removed from the playing board.

... ...

So that's when Lee's army became of less importance as an objective point and using the Army of the Potomac to uncork the trapped Butler took on a greater significance.

... .

That's true, at least Sherman, your hard hitting right wing, was making some headway. But looking back today it still seems criminal that the Army of the Potomac had had to endure those titanic bloodlettings against an unfettered Lee simply because of the incompetence of a few minor players.

The great plans which you had put into action in May were worthless by the middle of June. Sherman was still advancing, but at a snail's pace. As June ended, his army had not yet crossed the Chattahoochee River; he was still thirty miles from Atlanta, mired in front of a hill called Kenesaw Mountain.

....

You're right, General. It's time to stop talking about plans and get back to what really happened. In the world as it existed on June 13th, 1864, Butler was soundly bottled up along the James River; Meade was about to pull the Army of the Potomac out of the Cold Harbor trenches; Jubal Early was on the prowl in the Valley near Lynchburg; and Sherman was slowly but surely tightening the pressure on Johnston in Georgia. Does that about summarize it?

... .

Good! Despite all of this going on, your attention was focused on the movement to Petersburg and it had to take your full attention. This movement has been touted by many military experts as one of the great frontal shifts in the history of warfare. In effect, you were offering Lee the opportunity to hit the Army of the Potomac while it was on the move --- the very advantage *you* had been seeking since the armies started south.

... .

I don't think that I've overstated things, General. The Army of the Potomac was, in many places, only a few yards from Lee's troops. The army had to be withdrawn unnoticed and moved through the same swampy terrain which had thwarted both McClellan and Lee in 1862. Once free of the Rebel army and the swamps, the Union force had to marshal at the James River, then hotfoot it across a twenty-one hundred foot pontoon bridge --- and, just to add a little spice to the picnic, the whole affair took place deep in the enemy's country. Every minute was fraught with the danger that Lee would detect the move and come sweeping out of his Cold Harbor trenches to push the Union army into the James River.

The incredible fact was that the Union army was gone from Cold Harbor for three days before Lee comprehended exactly what was happening. Now you may feign all the modesty you like, General, but this move to the south bank of the James was not a casual Spring stroll in the Virginia countryside. ... .

You'll grant me then that it was a prodigious undertaking. Now let me ask you, as you stood on the south bank of the James River, is it fair to say that you thought that you had such a jump on Lee that the war was about to end? ... .

You really believed that you finally had an advantage over the Army of Northern Virginia; however, it would not necessarily bring the end of the war. You expected that there would be a good deal more fighting because so many factors entered into the equation: Could Lee get away from Richmond with a significant part of his army intact? If he were successful in joining forces with Johnston, could they overwhelm Sherman before the Armies of the James and Potomac arrived? You felt that the idea of Lee quitting just because he had lost a battle was highly unlikely. The question was not that the war would continue but for how long and what shape would it take. ... .

So you do remember saying to your staff that you thought it well to get across a great river and attack Lee before he was ready; but, as you say, the opportunity became another disaster. The back door to Richmond, through the railroad center of Petersburg, was wide open. Two corps of Union infantry were gaping at the open door, but, as if Dante's inferno were waiting for them beyond the portal, Smith and Hancock just couldn't muster the nerve to to order the men in. A day later

Lee had slammed the door and Meade's wildest tantrums as well as another ten thousand casualties couldn't pry it open again. Beauregard, who commanded at Petersburg until Lee came on the scene, maintained that had the Union high command sent a single corps on a swing to the west side of town, it would have entered Petersburg unchallenged. He had bet his whole defense on massing his few ragged troops in the eastern trenches and he won his bet.

... .

That *was* the last chance, wasn't it? Beauregard had won all the marbles and the war would continue for eight more months.

.. ..

Oh, that's right, Sir. There was one more opportunity to end the siege --- that was the explosion of the mine and the ensuing Battle of the Crater. Once again the leaders of the Army of the Potomac had been given a golden chance to break Lee's line. In your own words: "Thus terminated in disaster what promised to be the most successful assault of the campaign." That was fine to say in retrospect, but what chance of success did you anticipate when Colonel Pleasants and his Pennsylvania miners began to dig? I remember that you later wrote something about the work on the mine being approved "... to keep the men occupied." You had used this trick before the great campaign at Vicksburg --- or at least you said that that was the purpose of some of those wild schemes. You had also seen mining operations before. McPherson had engineered such a blast during the Vicksburg siege, but little had come of it. Are you sure that you didn't really expect very little to come from this enterprise, too?

... ...

You're telling me that you *did* take the mine seriously. As you saw it at the time, it offered the only chance to break Lee's

Richmond-to-Petersburg line. You also felt it was imperative to keep pressure on Lee --- an offensive threat which would prevent him from peeling off a part of his force to reinforce Johnston or Early.

....

So, you still think that the capital city defenses were so formidable that Lee easily could have shipped off several divisions and not sacrificed an iota of security.

I'm not completely convinced, General, but when I study your orders to Meade, I may have to give you the benefit of the doubt. It does appear that you regarded the mine as an opportunity for a clear opening to Lee's rear. As part of a series of stratagems, you moved II Corps and Sheridan's cavalry north of the James. Lee was certain that a major attack was brewing on the outskirts of Richmond some twenty-five miles from the mine; he responded by moving sixty percent of his available strength to the northern defenses. With Lee's move completed, you then ordered Hancock and Sheridan to surreptitiously recross the James and to be prepared to support Burnside's IX Corps in the attack.

....

"Surreptitiously" may be a ten dollar word, General, but what else would you call it. You went so far as to put hay on the pontoon bridges to muffle the sounds of men and horses on the march. To me that's "surreptitiously."

....

You insist then that you really did think that the mine was a good idea. You did speak well of the planning, but you didn't say the same for the generals assigned to carry out the plans. As you said later: "The only further precaution which [Meade] could have taken, and which he could not foresee, would have been to have different men to execute them. The explosion of 8,000 pounds of powder in the mine put a hole in

Lee's lines which was 170 feet long, 70 feet wide, and 30 feet deep. Burnside had a gap 500 yards wide to march his corps through and then into an undefended Petersburg less than a mile away."

....

You're satisfied, then, that Meade gave sufficiently explicit instructions to Burnside to get the job done. It's interesting what you said about these preparations: "All [the corps commanders] were to clear off the parapets and the abatis in their front so as to leave the space as open as possible, and be able to charge the moment the mine had been sprung and Burnside had taken possession. Burnside's corps was not to stop at the crater at all but push on to the top of the hill [beyond] the crater ... supported on the right and left by Ord's and Warren's corps.... Burnside seemed to have paid no attention whatever to the instructions, and left all the obstructions in his own front for his troops to get over the best way they could."

You continued that Burnside had picked Ledlie's division to lead the assault and you implied that a worse selection could not have been made. "Ledlie," in your opinion, "besides being otherwise inefficient, proved also to possess disqualification less common among soldiers." Even twenty years after the battle you still couldn't bring yourself to criticize a colleague outright, no matter how lowly your opinion of him may have been. The fact was, and you knew it, that Ledlie had been accused of cowardice --- of hiding in a bombproof (and some witnesses have added "... plying himself with rum ...") while his leaderless troops milled around the bottom of the crater for over an hour. In that hour the Confederates were able to recover, bring up replacement troops and artillery, and then enjoy the day as if they were at a shooting gallery.

Confederate General William Mahone, who took command of the troops who met Burnside's feeble advance, later noted: "After the explosion there was nothing on the Confederate side to prevent the orderly projection of any column through the breach which had been effected, cutting the Confederate army in twain ... opening wide the gates to the rear of the Confederate capital."

... .

You're serious, aren't you? You really do believe that the explosion of the mine was one of the great opportunities for shortening the campaign against Lee. It's clear from what you reported to General Halleck that you were extremely disappointed with the results: "This was the saddest affair I have witnessed in the war." To Meade you said: "So fair an opportunity will probably never occur again for carrying fortifications."

... .

Yes, I guess that does say it all. Another disastrous example in this bloody campaign of missed opportunities. Four thousand more casualties which in the end brought victory no closer. The war probably would have ended in the Spring of 1865 whether there had been a Battle of the Crater or not. At the hearings held by the Congressional Committee on the Conduct of the War (yes, General, there are still such committees --- only the name is different), you blamed the entire chain of command for the failure: "I think the cause of the disaster was simply the leaving the passage of orders from one to another down to an inefficient man. I blame his seniors also for not seeing that he did his duty, all the way up to myself." That was very noble of you to share in the blame --- and I must say not dissimilar to what one hears today when a misfortune of the same magnitude occurs. But how unfortunate it is that those soldiers of all wars who paid the ultimate price to compensate for the incompetence of others can't simply be recalled to life.

....

That's right, General, there was plenty of blame to go around. Meade and you had approved the idea; however, when it came time for the miners to do the work not much help was forthcoming from the Army of the Potomac. Sandbags, wood for beams, wheel barrows, surveying equipment and other needed implements had to be scrounged. The final ignominy was that even the fusing material which was used to set off the explosion was fashioned from scrap.

....

Correct, Sir! That's exactly what happened. The fuse failed at a splice and had to be relighted. With the entire Army of the Potomac at the ready, the explosion was delayed for an hour. As you say, you had other concerns --- Jubal Early, for instance, was roaming about the outskirts of Washington and Hunter was lost somewhere in the mountains of West Virginia; Sherman was finally tightening the noose around Atlanta while Confederate General John Hood vigorously attacked him at every opportunity --- besides checking every detail of how very experienced major-generals were preparing for an attack.

Nevertheless, this army was no longer a stranger to you and you had sensed that proper leadership had been its problem since Bull Run. That's why you had decided to remain with the Army of the Potomac --- to be sure that its generals did what you wanted done: *Follow Lee.* Early in the campaign, in utter frustration over the slow reflexes of the army's chain of command you had pleaded with your former aide to help you to understand: "Wilson, what's wrong with this army?" you cried and he shook his head without answering.

Throughout the three months of campaigning you had seen the lethargy --- the painfully slow march through the Wilderness, then Burnside's delayed arrival wiped out a chance to damage Lee's army before Longstreet's Corps joined the battle. At Spottsylvania it was Warren who dillydallied and Hancock's opportunity at the "Bloody Angle" went flying. At Cold Harbor both Smith and Hancock were late because a staff aide made an error and then the corps commanders neglected to reconnoiter their attack zones. Finally, in front of an undefended Petersburg, Smith and Hancock were unable to get their act together before Lee's men filled the trenches.

Lincoln understood. It was on a different matter, but he advised you "... it will neither be done nor attempted unless you watch it every day, and hour, and force it." You were surely aware that only when you showed a personal interest and remained on the spot did something get done.

.... ?

Yes, I do believe that's what happened at the crater. Meade also thought of it as a job for keeping troops busy, his engineers scoffed at the plan as a folly, and if they had even a hint that you were unconcerned poor Colonel Pleasants and his miners were going to get precious little support from on high.

....

That's true. Burnside *was* all for the plan, at least up to the day before the big shoot-off. Then he dropped not only the ball but also the bat and glove. Some good may have come from the four thousand casualties after all. The cowardly Ledlie was dismissed from the service and finally poor old ineffective Burnside was removed from active command. He wound up in a fitting place, however, the United States

Senate. Slowly, but inexorably, attrition was changing the complexion of the leadership in the Army of the Potomac.

... .

Well, General, you may not have thought that Burnside was so terrible. I know that you and he were friends after he had become a senator, but tell me, would you really have wanted him in command of IX Corps when Lee attacked Fort Stedman in March of 1865? I thought not.

That fairly well closes out the action around Petersburg until the Spring of 1865. For the next eight months the Armies of the Potomac and the James kept extending their lines to the west, moving toward the last railroad line which supplied Richmond and forcing Lee to stretch his lines to the breaking point. The action had shifted to the other theaters: Sherman took Atlanta and began his march to the sea; Sheridan dismantled Early's force in the Shenandoah Valley; and in December of 1864, "Pap" Thomas destroyed Hood's army at Nashville --- after you had almost replaced him for not being aggressive enough in attacking the fiery Hood.

... .?

Yes, General, it may have taken longer than you hoped, but the outcome *was* just about what you had planned back in the Spring of '64. Meade held Lee in a vise and the other armies were able to rip the Confederacy to shreds. By the end of September, the people of the North could feel victory coming. Then, in November, they made victory a certainty by reelecting Lincoln.

Lee also could feel the end approaching. In June he commented to Jubal Early that he had to destroy your army before it reached the James River. He then added: "If [Grant] gets there, it will become a siege, and then it will be a mere question of time." It happened as Lee said it would and when the siege ended in 1865, the homely name of a country crossroads town took its place forever in the book of legends.

The next time we meet, General, we'll take a look at the roads leading west to Appomattox Court House.

... ...

Thank *you,* General --- and you have a good day, too.

CHAPTER NINE

"... I WAS STILL SUFFERING FROM THE ... HEADACHE; BUT THE INSTANT I SAW LEE'S NOTE I WAS CURED."

The Road to Appomattox
(April 1 - April 9, 1865)

SYNOPSIS: Lincoln had been reelected, Sheridan was returning from the Valley to Petersburg, Sherman was marching through Georgia, and Thomas's Army of the Cumberland met and defeated the Army of Tennessee for the last time. As 1865 dawned, only Lee remained as a potent adversary; however, Grant did not consider the war ended. General Johnston had collected a scratch force in North Carolina. If Lee ever got his Army of Northern Virginia --- even as decimated as it then was --- combined with Johnston's band, the war may have gone on indefinitely. Grant's great fear was that he would awaken some morning to find Lee's trenches empty --- just as on that day the previous June, Lee had found the Army of the Potomac's lines empty at Cold Harbor.

When Lee did finally make his break, Grant turned to Sheridan again to harass the fleeing Rebels. The tension made Grant ill --- the return of a chronic migraine headache which seemed to afflict him at critical moments. The hierarchy of the Army of the Potomac (with the exception of General Meade) had undergone a complete turnover and with the new blood the army performed as it never had before. It finally hemmed Lee in at a small junction town in southwestern Virginia called Appomattox. When Lee offered to discuss surrender terms Grant's headache miraculously faded. For practical purposes the war was over.

... .?

Why, General, this is Appomattox Court House. Does it look that much different today?

....

In that way it's *much* different than it was in 1865. The whole town is now a museum so there's no children playing in the streets, no barnyard animals around, no horses tied to hitching posts. Oh, I can see why it would look strange to you, all right. But one part is the same. You can still see General Longstreet's trenches on the outskirts of town and ...

....

Yes, your old friend, Pete, had a big part in the war from the beginning to the end. I remember your saying that he was at your wedding, a close friend when you were in the old army and one of the Confederate officers with whom you kept in touch after the war. Everyone is now aware of his dispute with Lee over tactics at Gettysburg and I suspect that a lot of the support for your comments about Lee came from discussions you had with the "Old War Horse" (as Lee affectionately called him) after the war. At Appomattox, however, you were not facing your old friend. Even though he had seen Ewell's Corps collapse at Sailors Creek and he had heard Lee cry out with grief for his disintegrating army, he was still the number one corps commander in the Army of Northern Virginia. When Lee gave the order, he would be ready, if not willing to fight.

Now. General, what have you to say about the end of the siege at Petersburg and the Union armies' relentless pursuit of Lee to this little backwoods hamlet.

... .

So, you thought that the war was just about over in late March --- but once again you had mistakenly thought that only your forces would be on the offensive. As it happened, you

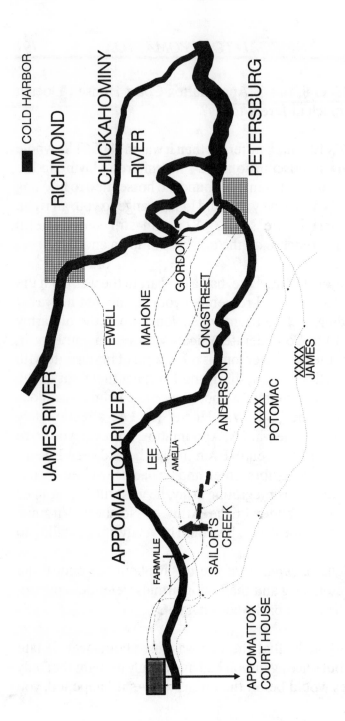

COLD HARBOR

RICHMOND

CHICKAHOMINY

RIVER

PETERSBURG

JAMES RIVER

APPOMATTOX RIVER

EWELL

MAHONE

GORDON

LONGSTREET

ANDERSON

XXXX
POTOMAC

XXXX
JAMES

LEE

AMELIA

SAILOR'S
CREEK

FARMVILLE

APPOMATTOX
COURT HOUSE

PURSUIT TO APPOMATTOX
APRIL 3 TO APRIL 9, 1865

were shocked when the lines suddenly erupted on March 25th as Lee threw everything he could muster into what he hoped would be a knockdown, if not a knockout, blow against your Petersburg line. His plan embraced your greatest fear --- that the Army of Northern Virginia would slip away like a thief in the night to join the Rebel armies in the deep South.

Lee had his own problem, however. He needed Jefferson Davis's approval before he could abandon the capital. After months of pleading, Davis finally had to agree with Lee that for the South to continue the war, the Army of Northern Virginia must be allowed to abandon the Richmond-Petersburg trenches. Once decided, it then became Lee's task to find an opening through which he could engineer his escape.

Over the winter the Army of the Potomac had been extending its lines further and further west. Lee was so hemmed in that he had little chance of maneuvering his army into a position for an escape run; he had to compel you to shorten the Union lines. The spot he chose was Fort Stedman, not far from where the Battle of the Crater had been fought seemingly eons ago. It was the point at which the two lines were closest and offered, therefore, the greatest possibility of surprise.

....

So you still remember that week. You issued orders on the 24th of March for a Spring movement, the day before Lee struck. What's that old saying about great minds running in similar channels ? You just described a perfect example. Lee assigned almost half of his army to the assault, about twenty thousand troops under General John Gordon and they rolled over Fort Stedman splitting IX Corps in two. Burnside's replacement, General Parke, was quick to respond and Gordon's attack faltered badly. The Army of Northern Virginia just wasn't the coiled spring it had been only a year before. By noon the break in the Union line had been restored and Gordon's Corps left almost four thousand dead, wounded or captured within the Union lines. Lee's last gamble had rolled out snake eyes.

... .

So, General, you think that the way the Confederate attack fell apart after its initial success was a good indication that the Army of Northern Virginia was already dead and all that was needed for the world to see its terminal condition was some good spring weather.

... .

Yes, Sir, there were signs of decomposition all around it. Over the winter, Sheridan's Army of the Shenandoah had virtually eliminated Jubal Early's corps as any sort of an effective force. That cost Lee about ten thousand irreplaceable men.

... ...

Yes, he lost another four thousand at Fort Stedman. His once mighty and seemingly invincible army had dwindled to, perhaps, thirty thousand capable soldiers.

... .

I'm sure that you were anxious to get the Spring campaign underway. You suspected that Lee, the consummate military man that he was, understood that even the great symbol of Richmond eventually would have to be abandoned.

....

And, as you say, you could not count on Jefferson Davis to ignore military principles forever, so you were anxious to get your troops moving before the day came when you would awaken to find Lee's trenches empty.

... .

Yes, your instructions to your corps commanders really did make your anxiety clear. The troops were to have their haversacks packed and be prepared to move out on a moment's notice. But Lee had lost his chance to elude you once his lance had been broken at Fort Stedman. Instead of loosening the noose as Lee had hoped, you drew it tighter.

Sheridan, one of the few generals in the Eastern Theater whom you trusted implicitly, had returned from the Valley. To Sheridan, therefore, you gave command of the movement against Lee's right rather than the more senior General Warren.

....

No, General, I didn't forget the special instructions which you gave to Sheridan --- I can readily understand why you would not want to give such orders, even verbally, to Warren. More than any other general, Sir, *you* had a feeling for the psychological side of war in a democratic society. You were well aware that the people of the North were war weary --- a defeat, even if it were just a perceived defeat, at the hands of Lee would have had a devastating affect on the home front. Sheridan was instructed to win a clear cut victory or to make the entire movement appear that it was just a cavalry raid heading toward the Carolinas.

... ...

I understand completely --- you simply had lost confidence in General Warren. You mentioned on several occasions that early on you had thought very highly of Warren; however, his constant dilatoriness and flow of excuses had worn on both you and Meade. Perhaps you did not want to disgrace an officer who had built a fine record this late in the game --- but for certain, fine record or not, you were not about to let Warren and his imagined fears allow Lee to slip from the trap which had been almost a year in the building.

So Sheridan had the hammer. You gave him the authority to remove Warren from command of V Corps if he thought it necessary. At a critical moment. Sheridan so thought and, rightly or wrongly, Warren was gone.

....

So now you think that Sheridan may have been too hasty in his dealings with Warren? You didn't seem to feel that way back in March of 1865. Warren made his appeal to you, but the war went on to its climax at Appomattox without him. Clearly, too much was at stake for you to enter into a bickering contest between generals. Warren's war was over.

....

Ah! There's the truth of it. You were just as happy that Warren was gone. You felt that the chase after Lee was going to require hard marches and stern leadership. Warren had displayed neither of these traits between the Wilderness and Petersburg.

... .

So, that's what happened. Warren was hours late in getting all of V Corps moving toward Sheridan's position at Five Forks. Well into the afternoon units of his corps straggled to the battle scene, but Warren himself had not arrived. Sheridan felt that it was imperative to strike Pickett before nightfall or the Army of the Potomac would have lost another golden opportunity for a tactical win. As you say, these were the relatively short days of early Spring, timing was crucial.

It is interesting how you later reported these events --- so succinctly that you seem to be saying that with Warren gone victory was assured: "Sheridan issued an order relieving Warren and assigning Griffin to the command of the 5th Corps. The troops were then brought up and the assault successfully made." You wrote of Warren later: "He was a man of fine intelligence, great earnestness, quick perception, and could make his dispositions as quickly as any officer, under difficulties where he was forced to act." Then your pertinent beliefs came to the fore: "He could see every danger at a glance before he had encountered it" --- sounds like the old Army of the Potomac syndrome to me and it must have sounded the same to you. You continued: "... as much as I liked General Warren, now was not the time when we could let our personal feelings for anyone stand in the way of success...."

....

Yes, Sir, that's true. The senior officer changeover for both the Army of the Potomac and the Army of the James was almost one hundred percent. Only Meade still held his job. General Humphries had replaced the ailing Hancock in II Corps, Wright had taken command of VI Corps after Sedgwick had been killed at Spottsylvania, Parke went in for Burnside after the latter had muffed the play at the crater, and now Warren. In the Army of the James, Butler of all people had fired Quincy Gillmore for inefficiency and then, with the election over and Democratic votes no longer important, General Edward Ord replaced Butler. Old "Baldy" Smith, an officer of whom you once were proud, finally complained his way right out of the army. Generals Weitzel (the general who *actually took* Richmond --- not Grant) and John Gibbon now commanded XXV and XXIV Corps respectively. The slate had been swept clean.

After Five Forks, you sent the Union armies against Lee's trenches for the last time and when the whirlwind hit, Lee knew that the jig was up. He had the choice of letting his once mighty Army of Northern Virginia die in the redoubts around Richmond or make an attempt to join forces with Joe Johnston.

....

Certainly you could see that he had only these choices and you had no problem anticipating what a general like Lee would do. The race for Appomattox Court House was on. At dark on April 3rd, Lee fled from Richmond. Before dawn you knew that he was gone and you sent Sheridan driving his cavalry west to prevent the resourceful Lee from turning south.

... ...

Yes, it looked as though everything was going according to plan, but, as you say, with Lee anything was possible. It almost came unglued when Meade and Sheridan disagreed on how to conduct the pursuit. They never had been on the best of terms and at this juncture their respective positions were peculiar at best. Technically, Sheridan was the Cavalry Corps commander and subordinate to Meade. Actually, he was your alter ego at the cutting edge of the pursuit. Lee had been moving relentlessly west, hardly pausing to rest his bone-weary troops or to pass out the meager rations which were available. Sheridan saw this; Meade didn't. Meade was on the brink of slowing the whole army down to attack a rear guard.

... .

So that's when Sheridan surreptitiously sent that message to you: "I wish you were here yourself," it read, "I feel confident of capturing the Army of Northern Virginia if we exert ourselves. I see no escape for Lee."

... ...

Of course you were quick to sense its desperate tone. You thought of the many times "fair opportunities" had gone up in smoke over the past eleven months. This time, if the opportunity were lost, you were going to be sure that it was not because some subordinate didn't get a job done. Even though it was after dark when Sheridan's message arrived, you immediately began the sixteen mile trek through the enemy's country to reach Meade and Sheridan. Your party rode through the pitch black darkness, getting to Sheridan's camp after ten that night. Having avoided the enemy's patrols, you were most fortunate that the Union pickets didn't dispute your passage. As you said: ".... and after some little parley convinced the sentinels of our identity we were conducted in to where Sheridan was bivouacked."

... ...

Right, Sir, after your little talk with Meade, he got the picture. The idea was not to chase Lee across home plate; rather, the Army of the Potomac should keep between Lee and his destination in southern Virginia or North Carolina.

... .

That's a good point, General, in fairness to Meade he was very ill at this point of the campaign --- actually running his part of the battle from an ambulance. We saw a similar situation with Lee at the North Anna and as he was unable to respond then, the usually reliable Meade didn't react exactly as you wanted in the pursuit. Then, it wasn't long before you became ill yourself as that god-awful migraine began its head-splitting drumbeat.

... .

Oh, you still remember that it struck shortly after the Union troops had overwhelmed the Confederates at Sailor's Creek and Lee sent his first message about terms of surrender. It was evident that the pressure was getting to you. In your own words, you could see that Lee's army was obviously crumbling, but you had been at the brink of victory before. You and Lincoln had discussed the impact another coup by Lee might have had on the war weary North --- all of the work Sherman, Sheridan, Farragut, and Meade had accomplished in the past year could have been undone in a single stroke. So, with the stress of battle, hours in the saddle, and even Lincoln urging you to "Let the thing be pressed," your body revolted.

... ...

You certainly were not well. This was one of the few times that you ever acknowledged that you were ill, and especially in such vivid terms --- you spoke of the mustard plasters, the foot soakings, the lack of sleep. You complained to Colonel Porter: "I am suffering too much to get any sleep." Then when Porter, who had a deep superstition about the timing of your headaches, asked if you were expecting some good news soon, you uncharacteristically replied, "The best thing that could happen to me today would be to get rid of the pain I am suffering." Do you remember any of it?

... .

I suppose that it would be hard to forget --- particularly the "as if by magic" cure. Lee's reply finally came --- he would meet with you to discuss surrender. You noted that it was precisely 11:50 A.M. when you received the message and later you wrote, "I was still suffering with the sick headache; but the instant I saw the contents of the note I was cured."

For a year you had been Grant the imperturbable, the unflappable, the core of iron who could accept any adversity with serenity, but your obvious feeling of concern when victory was imminent tells us something about you which seldom surfaced during your military career. The Army of the Potomac had broken the stalemate; however, you were convinced that the war would not be over until you had driven a stake into the heart of Lee's army. Now, with all the chips on the table and Lee trying to draw to an inside straight, you had to wonder if there might have been just one last wild card hidden up the master's sleeve. Am I wrong in guessing that you had all the human feelings of doubt and uncertainty that we all face at critical moments in our lives?

....

Yes, Sherman did say that you didn't have any trepidations when you went into battle, but this was no longer a battle --- it was pursuit. Let's remember that you had let both Beauregard and Bragg escape relatively unscathed after Shiloh and Chattanooga --- and you had been criticized for not pressuring their retreat more aggressively. As with those earlier victories, you had clearly won this campaign, but this time you could not let the enemy evade you. For Lee, merely to escape was to win.

... .

So, you do admit that you were really relieved and thankful when Lee called the bet and you knew that, at last, the game was yours.

... .. ?

No, General, no one would fault you for feeling apprehensive. Too many times you had seen victory fly away on the wings of indifferent leadership. And, even as Lee's army disintegrated before your eyes, you knew that there was still one thing that you had not accomplished during the bloody months since the Wilderness. That certain element which had assured success in all of your previous campaigns was missing --- you had not been able to dominate the will of General Lee.

... .

I have to agree with you on those points. You *had* beaten his army and the entire nation which Lee represented, but I'll say again that I don't believe that you had ever imposed your will on him. Surrender came because at Appomattox the Confederacy could give him no more chips for the game.

... .

No, General Grant, I seriously doubt that anyone ever claimed that Lee had dominated you either. You were always confident that in time you would win. But that doesn't mean that you didn't feel relief and elation when you finally received Lee's note and later heard Sheridan whisper, "Yes, he is in that brick house, waiting to surrender to you."

....

Yes, Sir, that's the McLean house over there. Would you care to say once more, as you said to Sheridan, "Well, then, we'll go over" and see what the place looks like today?

... .

No? You say that you've seen it before and that it would do you no good to look into that parlor again. I'm not surprised that you put it that way, General Grant. After all, you never did go to Richmond, did you? Back then you said to Julia, "... I think it would be as well not to go. I could do no good there, and my visit might lead to demonstrations which would only wound the feelings of the residents, and we ought not to do anything at such a time which would add to their sorrow." So, General Grant, the great conqueror, never did get to Richmond.

....

Of course you had more important things to do, General. The thrifty Ulysses Grant had to get to Washington to stop the War Department from spending that $3 million dollars a day.

CHAPTER TEN

PAPA GRANT, BOBBY LEE, AND OTHER GHOSTS FROM THE PAST.

The Desperate Need

SYNOPSIS: Grant was a far more complex individual than the history books usually portray. In short, he was the product of the 19th Century frontier --- a hard working farm boy with a domineering and verbally abusive father coupled with a nonnurturing, indifferent mother. Perhaps that is why he was at his best when his loving wife and family were nearby. It seems that they salved his desperate need for recognition and the warmth of love.

This background may have taught him at an early age to hide his true feelings. He has been often described as "Grant the imperturbable," but all his life there was a storm raging inside him. He seemed to record every slight that he ever endured in his psyche. We've seen his reactions to the unpleasantries in his youth, and in adulthood certain events also caused him to boil inside. For instance, the ill will between himself and General George Thomas was still evident some two years after the incident when Grant nearly (and unfairly) cashiered him for delaying his December, 1864 attack on General Hood. Likewise, in his writings it is clear that he considered himself the military equal of, if not superior to, General Lee. The fact that his compatriots and the wartime press never accorded him such honors irritated him until the day he died.

Rather than receiving accolades, Grant was frequently branded as an insensitive, bloodthirsty and unthinking dullard when the opposite was closer to the truth. He certainly was no dullard. He made his own battle plans, wrote his own orders, and his

MEMOIRS provide ample evidence of his straight thinking under extreme stress. He was called a "Butcher;"however, the fact is that the total casualties in the armies which Lee and Grant commanded over the four years of war were almost identical --- in fact, Grant's (despite his always being on the offensive) were somewhat fewer. The great difference between Grant and the other Civil War generals was that the losses his soldiers suffered ultimately led to Appomattox. The pragmatic Grant did believe that fighting was an integral part of war. His goal, therefore, was not to avoid fighting, but to make every drop of blood bring peace nearer. In the course of the war, he obviously made misjudgments which resulted in unjustified casualties; however, in his heart he believed that each attack he ordered brought the country a step closer to the end of the killing.

One of Grant's major faults throughout his life was his tendency to be too trusting of friends. Such gullibility made his Presidency a disgrace and nearly destroyed him later in life. Then, as he grew older, he lost his taste for the simple life --- he enjoyed being hailed as a hero worldwide and hobnobbing with the rich and famous. In fact, he not only wanted to associate with them, he wanted to become one of them. Neither he nor his wife could return to the simple village life of the Midwest; as life went on it was the bright lights of the East which attracted them and which led to his final tragedy.

Well, General Grant, we've come full circle. We're back at Galena, Illinois.

....

Yes, I do remember your once saying that all you wanted to do after the war was to return to Galena, be its mayor and have a sidewalk built from the railroad station to your house. It didn't quite work out that way, did it? After the war you visited Galena and found that the hero worshiping citizens had heard about your comment --- the sidewalk had been built before you had a chance to run for mayor. Then came eight years as President, the trip around the world, in all sixteen years had passed since you left Galena to muster-in recruits. Finally, you and Julia were back at this jumping-off point. Except for the sidewalk, Galena was still the same as it had been twenty years before; Julia and Ulysses Grant, however, were not. Within a few months, Galena slipped into history and the Grants established themselves in New York City.

Perhaps the little town on the Mississippi had too many ghosts; perhaps it was too difficult for the people of the town to reconcile their memories of a slouching, seedy leather store clerk whom they had hardly known, with the fact that this same person had become one of history's great warriors and the President of the United States. They must have wondered how they should react to such nobility. Is a slap on the back and the offer of a cigar --- most appropriate for a leather clerk --- the right thing to do with a hero? They were uncomfortable, and, although for different reasons, so were you and Julia.

It may well have been that the limited horizons of towns such as Galena were no longer enough for a couple who had received the acclaim of royalty and heads of state throughout the world --- a couple who had been immersed in the heady world of national and international politics. Julia, the well bred lady from the Missouri manor, had always had visions which carried her far beyond sleepy river towns and even your simple tastes had grown significantly since the victory at Fort Donelson. Let's be honest, you had found the world of wealth and privilege and had learned to enjoy it. Little wonder that these forces worked in combination to drive you away from your roots, and, like a stage-struck school girl, toward the Mecca of wealth, power, and prestige. It was on the Hudson, not the Mississippi, that you would recapture the glories of the conqueror and the President.

... .

I'll take your word for it, General. You agree that each of these factors played a part in your decision, but you maintain that your real interest in returning to the East was to be in the mainstream of activity --- something which was impossible in a small town.

....

Yes, we should remember that you were, if not poverty stricken, at least no longer wealthy. Your income from all sources was, in the dollar value of 1880, much less than you had earned as a major-general. Believe me, General, we today are well aware of the impact of inflation, particularly on retired people. Could it be that as you sat in that less than elegant house, a gift from the people of Galena, that you could still hear the scolding voice of Jesse Grant?

....

Yes, General, we know that he died in 1873; however, we also know that he had never changed his opinion that West Point had ruined his eldest son for the business world. Twenty years before he died he had warned you, "Now you are a general. It's a good job, don't lose it." That's why we wonder, as you surveyed your prospects in Galena, whether you could see his ghost still taunting you because you had never proved yourself in *his* world --- the world of business.

.... ?

Why all this interest in Jesse Grant? Simply because he was a shrewd businessman and also a bully. It could well be that his memory was a driving force in your life.

You were not a man of business. In your *MEMOIRS* you even told that story about your youthful failure as a horse dealer --- the time you told the seller both your first and final offerings at the beginning of the deal. Perhaps right there Jesse saw your natural instincts for business and decided that West Point and the army would suit you better than his tannery. Your brothers were never exiled to college; they joined him in the family business. But you, General, you he sent to West Point, whether you liked it or not. Do you remember that discussion? I almost called it an argument, but it never got that far, did it?

... .

That's it: "I won't go," you cried when told about the appointment. That carried no weight with Jesse the Bully. As you later wrote, "He said he thought I would, and I thought so too, if he did." When you, in desperation, called on him for help before the war, even Julia pointed out that he was anxious to help --- but in his own way.

... .

Well, if he was so pleasant and available to discuss problems with, how come that god-awful migraine was hammering in your head as you waited to talk to him about a job?

....

Of course we know about the headache --- and we also know that when you arrived in Covington you spotted your father on the street and went out of your way to avoid meeting him. Can you really say that you were comfortable with him?

....

No, you didn't appreciate going to Jesse and being forced to admit that you had failed --- not once but over and over. The Army, Hardscrabble, *Boggs & Grant,* county engineer --- a long string of bitter pills and now the head-splitting bitterest pill of all: To tell that self-made dilettante that you would be unable to provide for your family unless he helped.

... .

Oh, yes, he helped all right; and true enough that it was a most needed helping hand. But later, was there no end to what he expected you to do to reciprocate for his miserly $800 a year job? Instead of congratulating you outright on your promotion to brigadier-general, he tried to swindle a job for a business acquaintance. Did "Major-General Grant" impress him at all? I doubt it. Look at your own letter to Julia. You wondered whether the promotion. which was proof of the government's faith in your abilities, would convince your father that you were now able to sustain yourself. However, it was the power that a major-general wielded which interested him, not the fact that his son had achieved such an important position in the Army. Instead of offering congratulations, he tried to seduce you into joining him in supplying contraband cotton to Northern buyers.

....

Yes, General, that did cause one of the more distasteful actions of your military career. Because your father's partner in the cotton deal was Jewish you issued your vile order banning all Jews from your military district. Rawlins took you to task with all the vehemence of which he was capable and even your most stalwart supporter, Lincoln, silently rebuked you by rescinding the order without so much as a comment. It's unusual to hear you talk of that order. You had pretty well swept it under the rug and, like your alcohol incidents, filed it in your "never to be discussed" file.

....

I'll tell you exactly what I mean, at the time you simply dismissed the whole incident as a non-issue. You can't tell us, though, that such affairs and Jesse's attempts to secure an exclusive contract to supply the army didn't bring on more headaches? I think that the power Jesse tried to exert over you during his lifetime had a tremendous impact on how you felt about yourself.

... ...

No, General, I didn't mean that he had sapped your confidence. From that time in your youth when you had engineered a method of loading wagons alone --- a problem which had stumped all of the local experts --- you knew that you had a unique ability to master predicaments. You demonstrated this same ability in Mexico and when your regiment was trapped in the jungles of Panama. You proved it again and again during the war, didn't you? The problem was not really with you. Jesse Grant had saddled you with an excruciating cross to carry through life: "You were not he, if you lived to be a hundred you would never be the man he was; ergo, something had to be wrong with you." As you once said, your teachers made you repeat, "A noun is the name of a thing" so often that you had come to believe it. It seems probable, therefore, that Father Jesse (General James Wilson once described him as a close and greedy man with a nasty streak) missed no opportunity to inform you that you were the great disappointment of his life --- and you had come to believe it.

The truth is that you personally considered yourself a competent person who, with just the slightest bit of fortuitous circumstance (Don't scowl, sir, I didn't say luck) would have been the well-to-do farmer you had bragged about in California. But as failure piled upon failure even you began to wonder about yourself and, as you saw the look of pity in the eyes of your friends, the seeds of self-doubt became indelibly printed in your mind. That's why, as the war progressed and your fortunes had turned, as success begot success, it was not the adulation of the multitudes which you sought; it was a sign of approval from Father Jesse and those who had been so quick with pity which you so desperately needed.

... .

That's what I said, General. Almost the entire nation celebrated your successes; however, too often those whose approval you most desired simply turned their backs on you. ....?

All right, I'll name a few. We've already spoken about Jesse Grant. How about McClellan. Don't you remember that when you tried to see him in Ohio shortly after the war had started he had been downright rude? Then, after your victory at Fort Donelson, Halleck, McClellan and Buell treated you like a wayward schoolboy. I've also heard it said that the happiest part of being promoted to Lieutenant-General came from the realization that you clearly outranked Robert Buchanan of Fort Humboldt.

Look at how sensitive you were to criticism as you waited for the Spring and dry weather to come to Vicksburg. Little comments, such as the one about a newspaper being unfair to you, indicated the depth of your feelings.

Even after you had taken Vicksburg, chased Bragg away from Chattanooga, after Lincoln had named you to command all of the Union armies and the supercilious Halleck had become your clerk, there were still men --- men that President Lincoln had ordered to do your bidding --- who looked at you with that same pity in their eyes and with the simple statement, "That may be well; but remember, Bobby Lee is waiting across the Rapidan," rekindled those burning memories.

... .

You may say that I'm overstating the case, but look at how vehemently you reacted in the Wilderness when they advised retreating after Lee had hit the army's flank. Remember the "double somersault" tantrum?

....

You're darned right that I may have something. As a matter of fact, I believe that comments such as these were a big reason why you didn't particularly care for General Lee.

....

Please, General, let's have a little quiet, please. After all this is a peaceful neighborhood in a sleepy town. Now that you are calm I'll tell you why I say that Lee was not one of your favorites. An old politician (that's old to me, not to you. He ran for President some 60 years *after* your *first* election) used to say "Let's look at the record." When we look at the record we find that you had a deep felt belief that Virginia should not have joined the Confederacy. You maintained that you could understand how the people of South Carolina, growing up in the hotbed of secession, had been brainwashed by constant talk of rebellion; however, you could not understand why Virginians, who had never been exposed to the rhetoric of the fire-eaters, chose to leave the Union.

.... ?

It has plenty to do with General Lee, Sir. You were taking the people of Virginia to task for leaving the Union and, who was one of the leading citizens of that state? None other than Robert E. Lee --- and not only did he become a Confederate general, he accepted the position after he had refused General Scott's offer of Commander-in-Chief of the Union Army. So, General Grant, following your own logic path we see: Lee is a Virginian, educated at West Point and later its Superintendent, with thirty years of U.S. military service, applauded by General Scott as the most outstanding soldier on the continent; the conclusion must be that General Lee had no business supporting a cause which had the objective of tearing asunder the very concept of "*United*" States.

....

You should see my point. General. It's based on your own statements --- and I think that those statements were designed to convey a message. Let's look a little farther, and on a more personal level. Lee was your senior by some fifteen years, a colonel in Mexico when you were a lieutenant, what today we would call a father figure. As a matter of fact he was so much a father figure that a minor incident in Mexico still rankled you as you climbed the stoop of the McLean House to accept his surrender.

.. .. ?

Well, weren't you concerned that Lee would take your disheveled appearance as an affront? You seemed as nervous as a schoolboy that father figure Lee would again scold you for wearing a scrubby uniform just as in Mexico Colonel Lee had scolded the young Lieutenant Grant for being improperly dressed.

....

General, you may say that such a minor incident would never have bothered you, but in reality your sensitivities ran deep. For the record, when you wrote of Lee's surrender at Appomattox, you said that it was understandable that Lee, then Scott's Chief of Staff, may not have remembered much about a meeting he had had with you in Mexico. Nevertheless, it seems that you did feel somewhat chagrined when he added that, try as he might, he could not recall a single feature of your countenance. (When you recorded the incident in your *MEMOIRS* you omitted Lee's comment). Then, as the session dragged on, it was Lee who reminded you of the purpose of the meeting: To discuss surrender, not old times. It was as though it was not within you to bring the man down. Even some of your aides wondered which general was surrendering. It does seem that General Lee, the "Man of Marble," could eminently have filled the role first played by Jesse Grant.

... ...

I see your point, General, but let's look a little deeper. In one of our earlier conversations we said that you were able to defeat Lee's army but not Lee. This was far different from your other opponents. At Donelson, both Generals Floyd and Pillow ran away. At Shiloh, Beauregard threw apparent victory to the winds as he let your almost defeated army drive him into the safety of the Corinth trenches. At Vicksburg, General Pemberton could not even comprehend the whirlwind he had encountered; and after Chattanooga, Bragg made lame excuses to explain how his impregnable position had been overrun.

... .

No, General, I'm not trying to say that Lee got the better of you. In fact, you were the only Union general whom *he could not* dominate --- and he knew it from the Wilderness on. When you sent the Army of the Potomac sidling towards Spottsylvania, Lee fully realized that the tenor of the war had changed forever --- he would not have the power over you that he had had over your predecessors. He understood that to you Bobby Lee was not a legend to be feared, but only an obstacle along the way to victory.

... ...

No, Sir, I didn't mean that you underestimated Lee. You certainly respected his soldierly qualities and I believe that for the entire eleven months of the campaign there was not a day when you didn't worry that he might pull a military miracle out of his hat. What I mean is, despite your respect for his military capabilities, you felt he was very mortal and you resented the adulation the Union generals and the Northern press rendered to him.

... ...

General, stop putting words in my mouth. I'm not trying to imply that you resented the *respect* which others had for his abilities --- I'm talking about adulation. Let's go back to your own words to show exactly what I mean. How about: "The natural disposition of most people is to clothe the commander of a large army whom they do not know, with almost super-human qualities. A large part of the National Army, for instance, and most of the press of the country, clothed General Lee with just such qualities...."

Let's keep looking. On several occasions your writings indicate that the generally understood superiority of North-ern numbers was more myth than reality. You point out that the North had to guard its supply lines in hostile territory against the likes of Mosby, Forrest, and Morgan. You also argue that the methods of accounting for combatants differed in the two armies --- Union armies counted cooks and bandsmen; the Confederates only bayonets. By your calcula-tions, Lee, as he entered the Wilderness, had eighty thousand men in the Army of Northern Virginia --- not the sixty thousand with which he is usually credited. Moreover, none of this eighty thousand had to secure his rear areas. The result, as you totaled everything, was that your fabled adver-sary faced the Army of the Potomac with virtually no disad-vantage in numbers.

... .

General. I'm not arguing whether your conclusion is spe-cious or not; there is certainly a good deal of validity in your case. Union forces did dissipate as they moved into Rebel territory. However, when you repeat it so often twenty years after the war, it appears to be less a recollection of respective orders of battle than a challenge to those critics who main-tained that your conquest of Lee depended on the sheer weight of numbers rather than military skill. I particularly get this feeling when you follow a lengthy accounting of the armies' respective strengths with a downplaying of General Lee's performance from the Wilderness to the James River. You alleged that he was an austere man, inapproachable by his subordinates (I wonder who told you that?); nevertheless, you continued, he was extolled by the press of both South and North. This reporting, in turn, built the confidence of the Rebel soldiers and created fear in Lee's opponents. You further attribute the northern press's highly favorable treatment of Lee for the Union generals' attitude that you would be no match for the canny master. "Well Grant has not met Bobby Lee yet" became a phrase which burned within you until your dying day.

... .

Look, General, you may have had every right to have been irritated by their comments. I would also guess that you are quite correct when you say that the Union generals felt that your being called in from the West to take on Lee was a reflection on their own capabilities. That's why they played down the fact that your armies had conquered almost half of the enemy's territory, captured two enemy armies wholesale, and driven a third army in pell-mell retreat from an invincible position while the object of their adulation, despite stunning victories and eighty-seven thousand casualties, remained locked in a stalemate just a few miles from where the war began. I know that this explanation doesn't change the hurt you felt --- a hurt which still shows and ...

... .

I'm glad that you made that point, General. It's also something that you've said several times before --- you thought most highly of Joe Johnston's generalship. "One of the ablest commanders in the South," you once called him and you missed no opportunity to excoriate Jefferson Davis for failing to appreciate his skillful maneuvers against Sherman.

... .

Of course Davis's concept of strategy has always been one of your pet peeves; you never miss an opportunity to rip into him.

... ...

I think we all knew that you never meant to put Lee in the same category as Jefferson Davis --- rather you intended to put Lee's performance in perspective with that of other generals you had observed.

....

So, you still want to take one last shot at Jefferson Davis, do you? After all these years you still think that he may have been more at fault for the South's losing the war than were the Union armies. I have to say that your point makes sense. As you say, he tried to run both the government and the military (and apparently gave short shrift to both) until the final months of the war. When he finally turned the military reigns over to General Lee, the situation in the South was so desperate that we can't possibly measure Lee's capabilities as Commander-in-Chief. The only certainty is that Davis was a failure.

....

You're really on a Davis kick, General. Now you're saying that he was more than a failure --- you consider him to have been the most productive Union general. How do you arrive at that conclusion?

... .

All right, he interfered with Johnston at Vicksburg and lost both the city and the Rebel army; he visited Bragg and Longstreet at Chattanooga, helped to develop their plans and they both lost; he refused to form a consolidated command around Richmond until the Army of the Potomac crossed the James and he came within a hairsbreadth of losing his capital. You seemed to have proved your point General. I like your comment that "... on more than one occasion he came to the relief of the Union army ... by means of his superior military genius." But let's get back to the Lee situation.

... .

That's not the first time that you've said that most commentators seem to misinterpret your moves against Lee.

... .

Well, we discussed that just a while ago and I don't see...

... ... !

All right already, we'll go over it again --- briefly. You are saying that the purpose of the Wilderness and Spottsylvania fights was to keep Lee pinned above the Pamunkey River and thus let Butler, your attacking left wing, have a virtually free hand in the Richmond area. If Butler moved well and if Lee had to race to intercept a victorious Army of the James, Meade may have had an outstanding opportunity to hit Lee's army while it was on the move. Fine, we have accepted that.

... .

So your next point is that even if analysts ignore your overall strategic plan and concentrate only on the Army of the Potomac against the Army of Northern Virginia, they still should acknowledge that you did achieve several tactical advantages over Lee which should have brought better results. Faster action in the Wilderness might have crippled Hill's Corps completely before Longstreet arrived on the scene. A smoother move to Spottsylvania may have gotten the Army of the Potomac to the crossroad town before Anderson's Corps arrived there --- completely turning the situation about.

... .

So, you still believe that one of the reasons that the Army of the Potomac seemed to "just miss" after a crucial movement sprang from the ghosts of the Peninsula, Bull Run, Chancellorsville, and Fredericksburg --- mesmerizing the Army's generals whenever they so much as thought that Bobby Lee was in the vicinity. As you've said many times, the Bobby Lee of double somersault fame had them so panic stricken by thoughts of what *he* was going to do to them that they were incapable of concentrating on what *they* were supposed to do to him.

....

You do concede, though, that Lee had tremendous imagination and initiative which meant that his opponent had to be constantly alert. You concluded that the best way to keep Lee from exploiting *any* situation was to keep pressure on him.

....

You still argue then, that your attacks against Lee were absolutely necessary to keep him from sending a force against Butler, Sigel in the Valley, or even Sherman --- your order to Meade that Lee's army would be his objective point was your way of saying that Army of the Potomac had to keep the Eastern front hot.

....

That's right we saw what he did with Early when things quieted down after Cold Harbor. He sent General Early right to the outskirts of Washington.

.... ?

Yes, Sir, when you explain it that way it's hard to miss your point.

....

We agree, General, Lee was good, very good in fact, but neither was he a god. What I was trying to show. Sir, was that there seems to have been definite similarities between the events and people in your life which tended to unmask your well concealed sensitivities. For instance, your father ridiculing you for your lack of horse trading acumen, town boys making fun of your name, Colonel Buchanan forcing you to resign, General Halleck spoiling the fruits of your Donelson victory, the journalists who castigated you as a sluggard and a drunkard, or Lee, who, you believe, filched from you the everlasting glory which in your mind your wartime campaigns deserved.

General Grant, you were a far more complex man than your compatriots ever realized. They called you "The Sphinx" or the Quiet Man --- and outwardly, you were quiet. Inside, however, there was turmoil; the never ending search for recognition and approval. Peace seemed to come only when you were with your family and Julia was able to soothe you with her tender strokes.

For a while, you thought that you had made it. As you sailed around the world to fantastic acclaim, you had laid to rest all of the ghosts from the past. Then on your return, after the respite in Galena, you had the opportunity to move into the inner circles of the financial elite of the country. A new "Wizard of Wall Street," Ferdinand Ward, invited you to join him and your son Ulysses Jr.--- good old Buck --- as a partner in the thriving brokerage firm of *Grant and Ward.* A new start --- another chance to show the world the mettle of "Unconditional Surrender" Grant.

    .... ?

Yes, Sir, that will be our next stop: Wall Street, New York!

CHAPTER ELEVEN

*"I PROPOSE TO FIGHT IT OUT ON THIS LINE IF IT TAKES
ALL SUMMER --- AGAIN."*

1885, The Final Fight --- Against Poverty and Cancer

*SYNOPSIS: As we have seen, Grant was a master of predica-
ments and in 1884, as cancer of the throat drained the life from
his wasting body, he had his final opportunity to lay claim to the
title. In a few months he would die. Not only die, but die a
pauper and leave his widow destitute as well. Once more one of
his "friends" had played him for the fool and in the heady world
of high finance he had lost everything he owned.*

*He responded to an offer from Samuel Clemens (Mark Twain)
to write his memoirs for what seemed to be a fantastic sum of
money. He fought the cancer, completed the job and his effort
proved to be more successful than even the optimistic Clemens
had predicted. It not only reflected the same determination he
displayed at Spottsylvania when he proposed to "fight it out along
this line if it takes all summer," it was the fitting end to a warrior's
story.*

Here we are, General --- Wall Street in downtown New
York City. It certainly does look different than it did when
the firm of *Grant and Ward* had its offices in a building on the
corner of Wall and Broadway.

....?

Yes, that's old Trinity Church with the tall spire you could
see from your office window. It's still standing and its stained
glass windows and oaken doors continue to guard the street
which remains to this day the financial capital of the nation

--- and maybe the world. It was in the offices of *Grant and Ward* that you hoped to escape the everpresent spectre of poverty. You and Julia had been living high on the hog from the time the Civil War ended. The proceeds from the many financial gifts which a grateful nation had bestowed upon you as well as the savings from your $50,000 a year presidential salary had been largely used. Julia's penchant for entertaining royally; your hobnobbing with the likes of the Vanderbilts, Astors, Fishes, and Strongs; and the cost of the three year trip around-the-world had you on the brink of financial exhaustion. Julia moaned to her friends that her dear Ulysses was now poor and you both, not so whimsically, referred to yourselves as poor waifs.

... .

Oh, I understand very well why, after your globe-circling journey, you and Julia were once again at loose ends. I am well aware that there are few suitable jobs for ex-generals and ex-presidents. That's why the offer of a third term looked so appealing. Unfortunately, memories of the war were dimming and the people weren't quite ready to break the two term tradition. You needed a new beginning, not an easy task at age 62.

... .

Grant and Ward was to have been the new beginning, an enterprise which would have overwhelmed Jesse Grant's wildest dreams of success.

.. ..

A good point, General. The "Grant" in the firm's name was not that of General Ulysses Grant but Buck's name. *Grant and Ward* was doing well on Wall Street, but adding your name and prestige to the firm's executive board made Ferdinand Ward jump with joy. You invested all of your own assets plus over $100,000 borrowed from William Vanderbilt; with your contacts among the New York moneychangers, business at *Grant and Ward* was soon booming. Then, as in every business dealing which Ulysses Grant had ever tried, the world of *Grant and Ward* came crashing down. This time, however, it was not only financial disaster which you faced, this was a case of outright fraud with the concomitant flights from justice, criminal prosecutions and disgrace.

... .

That's right, General, I *am* talking about what you termed "the rascality of your business partner" which plunged you once again into the depths of financial despair. As you say, the world exonerated you, but the exoneration itself was as damning as Father Jesse's laughter. The only defense you and Ulysses Jr. could make was that you were two innocents who were incapable of understanding the heady world of high finance. At the age of 62, you were destitute --- and branded a fool.

....

Very true, General. This *was* worse than Galena. At least when you went to see your father for a job your debts were manageable and your personal honor wasn't on the line. In 1884, you had borrowed heavily to finance your partnership in *Grant and Ward* and borrowed even more in an attempt to keep the business afloat. Many of your friends and relatives made investments based on the strength of your name. Then Ferdinand Ward's schemes of pyramid payments and multiple loans guaranteed by a single security had wiped them out.

Do you remember May 5th, 1884, the day you realized that your sense for business was still as undeveloped as that of that little boy in Ohio who didn't know how to deal for a horse?

... .

I thought that you would --- it's been reported that you sought solace in the solitude of your office, stupefied by the chaos around you. In the war's darkest moments --- at Shiloh, Wilderness, or Cold Harbor --- you had never choked, but this was not the battlefield. You were in a world as foreign to you as China. While you sat at your desk, your head buried in your hands, I wonder if that headache was torturing you once more.

....

So, you don't really remember whether the headache was back --- you say that you had too many concerns about your family and the future to take notice of any pain. But didn't you know that you were the "Master of Predicaments" --- that you would, as you always had done when the chips were down, somehow find a way out of this situation?

....

Oh! I can imagine that it looked bleak to you as you sat in that dismal office, but soon you came up with the idea of writing about the war. Century Magazine had been begging you to write articles for them. You had always refused, but at $500 each, you felt that at least you could support your family and begin to make restitution to those who had suffered so grievously at the hands of Ferdinand Ward.

....

That's incredible, General, you mean that even the people at Century Magazine turned out to be petty swindlers. Your friend, Samuel Clemens (or Mark Twain if you prefer), maintained that even if they had paid *$20,000* for an article by U. S. Grant, they would have been robbing you. Clemens also knew that you had been approached by Century to write your memoirs and when he discovered that they were making offers like $30,000, he, at his vociferous best, branded them criminals. He knew that your memoirs would be the plum of the book world, whereupon he, the consummate businessman and newly incorporated book publisher, immediately offered you substantially more on the....

....

What? You still think that his offer of $50,000 plus royalties was too much for any book. Only you, General, the consummate *non*-businessman, would knock down a publisher's offer; he finally did press $20,000 on you --- and it came at a moment when there wasn't a penny in your pocket. Life took on a rosier hue; Clemens believed that your royalties might amount to more than $100,000. You were free once more, free from that seemingly everpresent apparition called poverty which hovered about you all of your adult life.

....

That was the final blow, wasn't it? Just when life seemed happy again, your Humpty-Dumpty world came crashing down. A bite of a peach, a feeling of rawness in the throat --- nothing to worry about, just a little summer cold. It will soon be gone. As you say, you had more important things to do than see a doctor for so small a malady. The summer at your New Jersey beach house drifted by pleasantly as you carved out Volume I of the *MEMOIRS*. It wasn't until October that the throat pain became so annoying that it forced a visit to the doctor.

. .. .

You recall every detail, don't you? A specialist, Doctor Douglas, was called in. His diagnosis: Cancer, well advanced. Once again the die was cast. Now, as you say, the work on the book was no longer a simple effort to provide an income for you and Julia. The memoirs were a way for you to redeem your honor and to provide a legacy for your *widow*. Writing the book took on the nature of a crusade as you pledged to finish the volumes before Death could have his way with you.

You and the family returned to your New York City home for the winter where, Fred, your oldest son and Adam Badeau, a wartime aide, joined you in the race to finish the book.

....

Yes, Sir, Badeau had written a book about your war experiences. *A Military History of Ulysses S. Grant* he called it. You always had cited Badeau's book as so thorough that it was unnecessary for you to write your own memoirs. Unfortunately, like many of your army compatriots, Badeau proved to be a false friend. He, perhaps, was worse than your other scurrilous acquaintances. They had used you strictly to satisfy their greed; Badeau was not only greedy, he wanted to filch that last vestige of dignity which you were so scrupulously trying to preserve.

Badeau started a rumor that he, not the inarticulate Grant, was actually the brain and the literary talent behind the memoirs.

....

That's true, General, you always gave Badeau credit for his assistance in writing the book. You had even expected that Badeau would finish the final editing of the text had you died before completing the final edition. But no one was about to steal this last chance for U.S. Grant to die an honorable and independent man. Amid the tremendous suffering as the cancerous tumor filled your throat and sent its tentacles burrowing into your neck, you happened upon a gossipy morsel in a New York newspaper which in no uncertain terms credited Badeau with being the true author of the book.

....

Yes, you certainly were at the brink of death in March of 1885. Your doctors had given up hope that you would even see the end of the month. Nevertheless the contemptible Badeau was dismissed. By the way, did you know that he later sued the family, but the case was thrown out of court?

... .

It happened after your death, so I didn't think that you were aware of it. As it happened, you didn't die in March even though the tumor had grown to monstrous proportions. It frequently hemorrhaged sending fountains of blood and sputum gushing from your tortured throat and you reported that a swallow of even the mildest liquid was like the passing of molten lead. As time passed, you could no longer even sleep in a bed. When prone the drainage from the tumor collected in your throat causing you to awaken with a convulsive retch. A huge chair became your permanent resting place. Despite these agonies, you knew that to preserve a shred of manhood, you, the lonely warrior, had to finish the book. With Badeau gone, the cause was yours alone.

....

Of course the doctors helped some, General, but medicine in 1885 was just coming out of the dark ages. They relied heavily on morphine and cocaine as well as direct injections of brandy. Therapeutically these accomplished little, but they did ease your pain. They also bathed you in a misty glow which may have skewed your memory somewhat and colored some of your final thoughts.

In the beginning you had dictated your comments and the words flowed with an easy rhythm. Each battlefield, each crisis came alive in your mind's eye and streamed onto the stenographer's page. Then your voice failed, and you had to write out all of your communications. Initially, you wrote the manuscript with the neat hand of a sternly switched schoolboy, but as the race neared the finish your penmanship became a barely legible scrawl. The pages themselves became graphic evidence of your suffering and sense of urgency.

....

I imagine that you *were* encouraged to continue when you found that your countrymen had not forgotten you. New

York's East 66th Street became a three ring circus as reporters from virtually every major paper in the country mobbed the area. The more enterprising rented rooms across the street so they could peer into your house to catch a glimpse of the dying hero. Silent sentinels, most of them former campaigners, stood guard or walked a somber post outside of your door. Each hoped to get a last peek at their living monument --- the man whose visage conjured up images of Donelson, Vicksburg, and Appomattox in the dreams of the aging soldiers. They waited through the winter and into the spring to be members of your final honor guard, but you made them wait in vain. They may not have known of the ferocious battle which was going on within you, but they would have understood. Decades before they had concluded that "Ulysses don't scare worth a damn." You had won for them then --- you wouldn't falter now.

The seasons passed and the work continued. In June the first volume went to the printer; the second volume, with Fred's help, was taking shape. Meanwhile. friends and relatives watched you waste away to a hollow shell. As summer came, the city's heat became unbearable. You and the family --- as well as the squads of reporters, curiosity seekers, and friends --- moved to upstate New York, to a new resort area called Mount McGregor.

There you sat on the most photographed porch in America as you continued to weave corrections and new ideas into the old words.

The reporters camped near the cottage, never wavering in their endless vigil. As in New York, admirers strolled by for that final glimpse of the hero of '65. The outpouring of public grief by the multitude seemed to buoy your spirits. You had once said, "When two armies seem played out, the one which can pull itself together for one last effort will prevail." That's what you were doing, pulling yourself together for that one last effort against the one opponent who, in the end, must always prevail.

You knew what the final result had to be, but you were going to parry his thrusts until *you* were ready to surrender. You understood that he would win the final battle, but the campaign victory was going to be yours. Your triumph came on July 14th; you declared that the work was finished and you saw that it was good. Solaced by your accomplishment you finally were able to rest. Less than a week later, at eight o'clock on the morning of July 20, 1885 the inevitable surrender came. ... . ?

Yes. General, the book did very well, both financially and literally. Julia received almost half a million dollars in royalties, an American record at that time. Even today, scholars and literary critics celebrate your *MEMOIRS* as a triumph. Few who read them today are aware of your suffering as you penned those final words since, through the mist of drugs and hurt, there emerges such a straightforward and understandable chronicle of this terrible epoch. To the end you preserved your title as the "Master of Predicaments."

Samuel Clemens (no doubt with a glance towards the sales receipts) maintained that the completed *MEMOIRS* rivaled Caesar's account of the Gallic Wars. The powerful and exact prose still arouses some Grant critics to question whether there was a ghost writer, but the experts who glory in ferreting out such discrepancies are quick to point out the similarity of style in your wartime reports and orders. They concede that the *MEMOIRS* unequivocally flowed from the hand of Ulysses S. Grant.

Most of all, the *MEMOIRS* told your story --- the story which would now be available to all generations of Americans. The story of a tanner's son who, like a Joshua, brought down the walls, not of Jericho, but of Donelson, Vicksburg, Chattanooga and Richmond. The story of the leather store clerk who vanquished those who threatened to destroy his homeland and thereby preserved the United States for its God-intended greatness.

General Grant, at Appomattox you embraced the concept "Let us have peace." The theme of your Presidential Inauguration speech was "Let Us Have Peace." The concluding thoughts in your *MEMOIRS* proclaimed "Let Us Have Peace," and above the monument that is your tomb, your countrymen inscribed the words "Let Us Have Peace." Let us hope, General, that you now have found that peace which seemed to elude you in life.

..... .

You said it, Sir. "Amen."

BIBLIOGRAPHY

_____. *Battles & Leaders of the Civil War*, four vols. New York: Century Company, 1884-87.

Badeau,Adam. *Military History of Ulysses S. Grant.* New York: D. Appleton and Company, 1885.

Catton, Bruce. *Short History of the Civil War.* New York: American Heritage Publishing Company, 1960.

_____. *U.S. Grant and the American Military Tradition.* Boston: Little-Brown & Company, 1954.

_____. *This Hallowed Ground*, New York: Doubleday & Company, 1955.

_____. *Grant Moves South.* Boston: Little, Brown and Company, 1960.

_____. *Grant Takes Command.* Boston: Little, Brown and Company, 1969.

_____. *A Stillness at Appomattox.* New York: Doubleday and Company, 1953.

_____. *The Coming Fury.* New York: Doubleday and Company, 1961.

_____. *Terrible Swift Sword.* New York: Doubleday and Company, 1963.

_____. *Never Sound Retreat.* New York: Doubleday and Company, 1964.

Cooke, General John Esten, C.S.A. *Wearing of the Gray.* New York: E.B. Treat and Company, 1867.

Copee, Henry, *Life and Services of General U.S. Grant.* Chicago: The Western News Company, 1868.

Dowdy, Clifford. *Lee's Last Campaign.* New York: Bonanza Books, 1960

Dupuy, R. Ernest & Trevor N. *Military Heritage of America.* New York: McGraw-Hill Incorporated, 1956.

Esposito, Vincent J. (ed.) *West Point Atlas of American Wars, Volume I,* New York: Frederick Praeger Company, 1959.

Fuller, General J.F.C. *Generalship of U.S. Grant.* New York: Dodd, Mead and Company, 1929.

_____. *Grant and Lee.* New York: Charles Scribner's Sons, 1933.

Grant, Ulysses S. *Personal Memoirs*, 2 Volumes. New York: Charles L. Webster and Company, 1886.

Lewis, Lloyd. *Sherman Fighting Prophet.* New York: Harcourt, Brace and Company, 1932.

_____. *Captain Sam Grant.* Boston: Little, Brown and Company, 1950.

Lee, Captain Robert E. *Recollections and Letters of General Robert E. Lee.* New York: Doubleday Page and Company, 1924.

Long, General A.P. *Memoirs of Robert E. Lee*. New York: J.M. Stoddard and Company, 1886.

McFeely, William S. *GRANT*. New York: W.W. Norton & Company, 1981.

Meade, George G. *The Life & Letters of George Gordon Meade*. New York: Charles Scribner & Sons, 1913.

Oates, Stephen B. *With Malice Toward None*. New York: Harper & Row, Publishers, 1977.

Porter, Horace. *Campaigning With Grant*. New York: Century Company, 1906.

Ropes, John. *Story of the Civil War*, 4 Volumes. New York: G. Putnam and Sons, 1894.

Sandburg, Carl. *Abraham Lincoln, The War Years*, 4 Volumes. New York: Harcourt Brace and Company, 1939.

Smith, Gene. *Lee and Grant*. New York: McGraw-Hill Book Company, 1984.

Symonds, Craig L. *A Battlefield Atlas of the Civil War*. Annapolis: The Nautical & Aviation Publishing Company, 1983.

Thorndike, Rachel Sherman (ed.). *The Sherman Letters*. New York: Charles Scribner's Sons, 1894.

Todd, Helen. *A Man Named Grant*. Boston: Haughton, Mifflin Company, 1940.

_____.United States War Department. *The War of the Rebellion: A* Compilation of the Official Records of the Union and Confederate Armies. Washington: 1880-1901. (Usually referred to as the Official Records or "ORs".}

Weigley, Russell F. *The American Way of War*. Bloomington: The Indiana University Press, 1973.

Wilson, James H. *The Life of John Rawlins*. New York: Neale Publishing Company, 1916.

_____. *Under the Old Flag*, 2 Volumes. New York: Appleton Company, 1912.

Woodward, W.E. *Meet General Grant*. New York: Horace Liveright, 1928.

Young, James Russell. *Around the World With General Grant*. New York: American News Company, 1879.

INDEX

Anderson, Richard H. L-Gen. CSA, 150, 160, 217

Antietam, 80

Appomattox Court House, 24, 47, 189, 190, 191, 196, 198, 201, 212

Army of Northern Virginia, 15, 122, 138, 141, 145, 147, 156, 164, 167-169, 170, 172, 174, 177, 178, 181, 190-194, 197, 214, 217

Army of Tennessee, 24, 134, 190

Army of the Cumberland, 24, 117, 118, 119, 120-127, 129, 131-133, 137

Army of the James, 137-138, 164, 172, 176-178, 181, 197, 217

Army of the Ohio, 82, 93

Army of the Potomac, 15, 73, 117, 118, 128, 137-138, 140-148, 150, 156, 160, 162, 164, 165, 166, 169, 170-179, 180, 182, 186, 193, 196, 197, 199, 200, 214, 218

Army of the Shenandoah, 194

Army of the Tennessee, 67-68, 72, 79, 81-87, 93, 94, 112, 117, 122, 125, 128, 129, 137

Atlanta Campaign (1864), 67, 137, 171

Badeau, Adam B-Gen. USA, 38, 224, 225

Banks, Nathaniel P. M-Gen. USA, 105, 113, 114, 137

Beauregard, Pierre G.T. Gen. CSA, 79, 83, 86, 89, 172, 179, 182, 201, 213

Belmont, Battle of, 38, 45, 61-62, 63-64, 97

Bermuda Hundred, Virginia, 138, 165, 179

Bragg, Braxton Gen. CSA, 24, 50, 93, 117, 118, 121, 122, 129, 131, 175, 201, 213, 216

Breckenridge, John C. M-Gen. CSA, 178

Buchanan, Robert C. L-Col. (later B-Gen.) USA, 33, 34, 35, 71, 74, 139, 210, 219

Buckner, Simon Bolivar L-Gen. CSA, 69-70

Buell, Don Carlos M-Gen. USA, 45, 50, 64, 71, 79, 82, 84, 86, 87, 88, 93, 123, 124, 210

Burnside, Ambrose E. M-Gen. USA, 128, 129, 134, 140, 146, 148, 149, 162, 183-185, 187, 188, 193

Butler, Benjamin F. M-Gen. USA, 42, 105, 134, 137, 165, 167, 176, 177, 179, 180, 197, 217, 218

Cadwallader, Sylvanus, 42

Chancellorsville, Virginia, Battle of (May, 1863), 80

Chattanooga, Tennessee, 93, 117
  Battle of (November, 1863), 24, 28, 67, 118-135, 201, 213, 216,

Chickamauga, Battle of (September, 1863), 24, 117, 118, 127, 128, 132, 175

City Point, Virginia, 171, 172

Clemens, Samuel (Mark Twain), 210, 223, 224, 228

Cold Harbor, Battle of (June, 1864), 28, 138, 139, 140, 143, 147,

160, 162, 165, 167, 168, 169, 172, 174, 177, 180, 181, 218

Corinth, Mississippi, 73, 81-82, 83, 87, 92, 118, 120, 213

Cumberland River, 68, 77

Dana, Charles A. (Asst Sec War), 39, 41, 42, 96-97, 106, 114, 119, 120

Davis, Jefferson, 97, 117, 128, 175, 193, 194, 216

Dent, Frederick (Grant's father-in-law), 51, 71

Dent Frederick, (Grant's brother-in-law & West Point classmate), 21, 22, 50

Donelson, Fort, 23, 28, 38, 41, 44, 45, 46, 61, 62, 65-70, 72, 73, 75, 77, 79, 81, 83, 84, 108, 113

Early, Jubal A. L-Gen. CSA, 166, 170, 180, 182, 188, 194, 218

Ewell, Richard S. L-Gen. CSA, 20, 142, 160, 191

Foote, Andrew H. R-Adm, USN, 40, 65, 66, 69, 70, 75, 108

Forrest, Nathan Bedford L-Gen. CSA, 100, 148, 214

Frémont, John C. M-Gen. USA, 37, 38, 44, 59, 60, 61, 104, 124, 178

Galena, Illinois, 36, 37, 52, 53, 54, 55, 71, 204, 205, 219, 222,

Gettysburg, Battle of (July, 1863), 80, 117, 118, 122, 134, 136, 146, 175

Gibbon, John M-Gen. USA, 197

Gillmore, Quincy A. M-Gen. USA, 138, 179, 197

Gordon, John B. L-Gen. CSA, 143, 144, 150, 193

Grant, Frederick Dent (son), 224

Grant, Hannah Simpson (mother), 21, 48

Grant, Jesse (son), 53

Grant, Jesse Root (father), 21, 48, 52, 63, 64, 70, 74, 104, 206, 209, 212, 221, 222

Grant, Julia Dent (wife), 21, 30, 34, 42, 50, 202, 205, 207, 224, 228

Grant, Ulysses S. General, USA,
  bankruptcy of, 222 et seq.
  business sense, 16, 25, 51, 222, 224
  childhood, 21, 47-49
  civilian life, 25, 35, 36, 52
  difficulties with superiors, 22, 33-35, 73-75
  drinking habits, 15, 22, 23, 27-43, 59-60
  in Galena, 53, 54, 59, 219
  financial security concerns, 219, 221
  "Hardscrabble," 51, 207
  marriage of, 21, 30, 50
  in Mexican War, 29, 49-50
  names and nicknames of, 21, 23, 29, 48, 71
  opinion of enemy generals, 50, 62, 211-216
  Pacific Coast activities of Captain "Sam," 22-23, 31-35, 51
  Presidency, 16, 25-26
  resigns from the Army in 1854, 22, 35, 51

Grant, Ulysses S., Jr.(Buck -- son), 31, 51, 219, 221, 222

Grant & Ward, 219, 220, 221, 222

Halleck, Henry W. M-Gen. USA, 38, 41, 44, 45, 46, 61, 64-69, 71-75, 79, 81, 87, 91, 92, 93, 96, 97, 100, 101, 112, 113, 114, 117, 121, 125, 142, 163, 173, 185, 210, 219

Hancock, Winfield S. M-Gen. USA, 148, 149, 156, 158, 160, 168, 172, 181, 183, 187,

Henry, Fort, Battle of (February, 1862), 23, 38, 45, 46, 65-66, 69, 74, 108

Hill, Ambrose Powell L-Gen. CSA, 143, 148, 149, 160

Holly Springs, Mississippi, 101, 103, 107, 108, 121

Hood, John B. Gen. CSA, 125, 186, 188, 203

Hooker, Joseph M-Gen. USA, 62, 118, 128, 129, 130, 131, 134, 138, 140, 143, 146, 150

Humboldt, Fort,
    Captain "Sam" Grant stationed at (1854), 34, 35, 36

Hunter, David M-Gen. USA, 104, 165, 167, 178, 186

Jackson, Thomas ("Stonewall") L-Gen. CSA, 143, 148

James River, Virginia, 137-138, 165, 171, 176, 180, 181, 215, 216

Johnston, Albert Sidney Gen. CSA, 50, 66, 79, 83, 86

Johnston, Joseph E. Gen. CSA, 50, 111, 121, 137, 144, 177, 181, 182, 190, 197, 215, 216

Knoxville, Battle of (November, 1863), 128, 129, 133,

Ledlie, James L. B-Gen. USA, 184, 187

Lee, Robert E. Gen. CSA, 15, 17, 20, 24, 47, 50, 70, 117, 134, 136, 137, 140-145, 150, 152, 154, 156, 158, 160, 162, 163-169, 178-183, 185-188, 190-202, 203, 204, 210-219

Lincoln, Abraham, 17, 19, 20, 23-25, 27, 36, 38, 39, 45, 47, 53, 59, 61, 71, 72, 74, 81, 86, 88, 89, 91, 92, 93, 96, 100, 105, 106, 108, 114, 118, 119, 121, 132, 135, 136, 141, 150, 171, 188, 190, 200, 208, 210

Livermore, Mary (Sanitary Commission Agent at Vicksburg), 41-42

Longstreet, James (Pete) L-Gen. CSA, 20, 122, 128, 132, 150, 160, 191, 216, 217

Lookout Mountain, Battle of (November, 1863), 129-131

McClellan, George B. M-Gen. USA, 22, 33, 38, 41, 44, 45, 50, 54, 55, 60, 64, 70-73, 92, 104, 124, 140, 146, 173, 174, 180, 210

McClernand, John A. M-Gen. USA, 56, 69, 87, 93-94, 96, 100-101, 104, 109, 113, 114

McPherson, James B. M-Gen. USA, 42, 86, 107, 124, 137, 182

Mahan, Dennis Hart, 116

Meade, George G. M-Gen. USA, 50, 136, 137, 142, 146, 148, 164, 167, 171, 172, 175-177, 180, 182, 183, 185-187, 188, 195, 198, 199, 217, 218

Mexican War, 53, 62

Mosby, John S. Col. CSA, 147-149, 214

Mount McGregor, New York, 227
    Grant's death at, 228

New York City, 205, 219, 220, 224

Ord, Edward O.C. M-Gen. USA, 120, 197

Paducah, Kentucky, 66, 77
    Occupied by Grant (September, 1862), 23, 38, 45, 60, 61

Pemberton, John C. L-Gen. CSA, 50, 102, 111-113, 121, 122, 125, 134, 213

Petersburg, Battle & Siege (1864-65), 169, 170-189, 191, 192

Pillow, Gideon J. B-Gen. CSA, 50, 62, 67, 69, 213,

Pleasants, Henry B-Gen. USA., constructs the Petersburg mine, 182, 187

Pope, John M-Gen. USA, 62, 71, 124, 140, 146

Porter, David D. R-Adm. USN, 42, 96, 103, 108, 109

Porter, Horace, B-Gen. USA, 141, 200

Port Hudson, Louisiana, 99, 108, 112, 113

Prentiss, Benjamin M. M-Gen. USA, 85, 88, 123

Rawlins, John A. M-Gen. USA, 36, 37, 40, 42, 109, 135, 208

Richmond, Virginia, 137-138, 147, 152, 167, 172, 174, 175, 176, 177, 181, 183, 193, 194, 198, 202, 216, 217

Rosecrans, William S. M-Gen. USA, 117, 118, 119, 120, 122, 123, 124, 127, 149

Scott, Winfield Brevet L-Gen. USA, 30, 44, 49, 53, 116, 211Sedgwick, John M-Gen. USA, 143, 197

Shenandoah Valley, Virginia, 137, 165, 170-71, 178, 188

Sheridan, Philip H. M-Gen. USA, 119, 123-124, 134, 170, 183, 188, 190, 194, 195, 196, 198, 199, 202

Sherman, William Tecumseh, M-Gen. USA, 16, 42, 45, 64, 67-68, 71-72, 75-78, 91, 105, 118, 123, 126, 129, 130, 131, 134, 142, 175, 177, 179, 186, 188, 190, 199
  credits Grant with recovery, 77
  at Shiloh, 84-87
  at Vicksburg, 101-112, 116, 121

conducts 1864 campaign against Atlanta, 104, 137, 171

Shiloh (Pittsburgh Landing, Tn.), Battle of (April 1862), 38-39, 72, 74, 75, 76, 77, 78, 79-95, 97, 123, 201

Sigel, Franz M-Gen. USA, 137, 178, 179, 218

Smith, Charles F. M-Gen. USA, 45, 69, 71-74, 79, 82

Smith, William F.("Baldy") M-Gen. USA, 42, 119, 128, 134, 138, 164, 167, 172, 179, 181, 187, 197

Spottsylvania, Battle of (May, 1864), 138, 139, 140, 147-160, 162, 167, 169, 173, 177, 187, 213, 217

Stanton, Edwin P. U.S. Secretary of War, 44, 46-47, 96, 100, 106, 118, 119, 120, 124, 174

Taylor, Zachary, General & President USA, 53

Tennessee River, 39, 66, 68, 77, 126, 127, 128

Thomas, George H. M-Gen. USA, 118, 120, 122, 124, 125, 130, 131, 134, 137, 188, 190, 203

Twain, Mark. See Clemens, Samuel.

Upton, Emory M-Gen. USA, 154

Van Dorn, Earl M-Gen. CSA, 92, 102, 103, 109, 116, 118, 120, 121, 123, 148

Vicksburg, Mississippi, 24, 28, 39, 43, 67, 73, 82, 93, 96, 121, 134, 166, 182, 213, 216
  battle of (May-July 1863), 97-117, 118
  Grant's attempts to bypass (December 1862-April 1863), 97-109

Wallace, Lew M-Gen. USA, 84, 88, 178

Ward, Ferdinand,
Forms Grant & Ward with Ulysses Grant, Jr. (Buck), 219
perpetrates security fraud, 222, 223

Warren, Governeur M-Gen. USA, 158, 160, 187, 195-197

Washburne, Elihu B. Republican congressman, 36, 40, 54, 59, 92, 119, 133

Weitzel, Godfrey M-Gen. USA., captures Richmond, 197

West Point, U.S. Military Academy at, 20, 21, 22, 46, 48, 49, 52, 54, 55, 63, 72, 76, 105, 125, 206, 207, 211

Wilderness, Battle of (May, 1864), 138, 140-146, 149, 152, 162, 169, 177, 187, 201, 213, 217

Wilson, James Harrison, M-Gen. USA, 144, 186, 209

Wright, Horatio G. M-Gen. USA, 158, 160, 197

Yates, Richard, Governor of Illinois (1861), 22, 54, 56, 59
    appoints Grant Colonel of Volunteers, 1, 23, 56

ABOUT THE AUTHOR

Thomas G. McConnell was born in Brooklyn, New York. He attended St. Francis Xavier High School in New York City, received his baccalaureate degree from Georgetown University, Washington, D.C. and his Masters from The George Washington University, Washington, D.C. After graduating from Georgetown, he entered the United States Air Force and retired in the rank of colonel in 1981.

Colonel McConnell was awarded the Air Force rating of jet fighter pilot. He flew 225 combat missions in fighter-bomber aircraft in Vietnam, served as an air division commander and closed his career with five years on the faculty of The National War College, Washington, D.C.

His responsibilities at the War College, a senior service school for high ranking officers from all services and selected government civilians, included being the course director for "Military Strategy to 1945." This course covered the history of warfare from antiquity to the end of World War II. A major portion of the curriculum was devoted to the American Civil War and included field trips to the Civil War battlefields. Since his retirement he has remained active in Civil War pursuits, campaigning regularly with the noted historian Dr. Jay Luvaas and his colleagues who constitute Dr. Luvaas's Civil War association, "The Army of the Cussewago."

Colonel McConnell and his wife, the former Patricia Joyce, have three sons (Patrick, Thomas and Kevin) and reside in the Virginia suburbs of Washington D. C.

(SAN: 200-3287)

ORDER FORM

Mail To: **Walnut Hill Publishing Co.**
7306 Masonville Dr.
Post Office Box 1395
Annandale, Virginia 22003-1395
Enclosed is a check/Money Order for _____ payable to
Walnut Hill Publishing Co.
Please send :
___ softcover copies @ $ 9.95
___ hardcover copies @ $19.95
of *CONVERSATIONS WITH GENERAL GRANT* by
Colonel Thomas G. McConnell, USAF (Ret).
SALES TAX: Please add 4.5% for book(s) shipped to Virginia addres-
ses. SHIPPING: $1.50 for the first book and 30c for each additional book.
___ I don't want to wait the 2 - 3 weeks it may take for book-rate mail .
delivery. Enclosed is $3.00 per book for First Class Mail or a rapid par-
cel delivery service.
___ Please send me information concerning quantity order discounts.
I understand that if I am not satisfied I may return the book(s) within
thirty days for a full refund.

NAME:_____ -
ADDRESS: _____
CITY: _____
ZIP:_____
DAY TIME PHONE: (   ) _____

ISBN: 1-878332-10-4 (softcover)
1-878332-11-4 (hardcover)

(SAN: 200-3287)

ORDER FORM

Mail To: **Walnut Hill Publishing Co.**
7306 Masonville Dr.
Post Office Box 1395
Annandale, Virginia 22003-1395
Enclosed is a check/Money Order for _____ payable to
Walnut Hill Publishing Co.
Please send :
___ softcover copies @ $ 9.95
___ hardcover copies @ $19.95
of *CONVERSATIONS WITH GENERAL GRANT* by
Colonel Thomas G. McConnell, USAF (Ret).
SALES TAX: Please add 4.5% for book(s) shipped to Virginia addresses. SHIPPING: $1.50 for the first book and 30c for each additional book.
___ I don't want to wait the 2 - 3 weeks it may take for book-rate mail delivery. Enclosed is $3.00 per book for First Class Mail or a rapid parcel delivery service.
___ Please send me information concerning quantity order discounts.
I understand that if I am not satisfied I may return the book(s) within thirty days for a full refund.

NAME:_____

ADDRESS: _____

CITY: _____

ZIP:_____

DAY TIME PHONE: (   ) _____

ISBN: 1-878332-10-4 (softcover)
1-878332-11-4 (hardcover)